Dress and Undress

Iris Brooke

DRESS AND UNDRESS

THE RESTORATION AND EIGHTEENTH CENTURY

GREENWOOD PRESS, PUBLISHERS
WESTPORT, CONNECTICUT

Library of Congress Cataloging in Publication Data

Brooke, Iris.
    Dress and undress: the Restoration and eighteenth
century.

    Reprint of the ed. published by Methuen, London.
    1. Costume--Great Britain.   2.   Costume--History--
17th century.   3. Costume--History--18th century.
I. Title.
[GT735.B68 1973]   391'.00942   73-3011
ISBN 0-8371-6829-5

First published in 1958
by Methuen & Co Ltd, London

Reprinted with the permission of Iris Brooke

First Greenwood Reprinting 1973

Library of Congress Catalogue Card Number 73-3011

ISBN 0-8371-6829-5

Printed in the United States of America

Contents

TO

Charles Wade

Introduction

THE purpose of this book is twofold. First to set out the groups of various garments of one period worn together or individually to suit their wearers' habits and requirements, and secondly to explain their construction for the benefit of stage designers.

The title may be misleading in its modern interpretation, but, during the period I am writing about, 'Dress' meant full dress and 'Undress' was an accepted term used for anything that fell short of full dress, formal 'deshabille' or informal utilitarian. Undress was worn in the morning, indoors and outdoors. To discard one part of a full dress, such as a hoop, a cravat or periwig, a coat or long gown was to be 'undressed'. Domestics, except on show occasions, always wore undress.

There were also a dozen garments made especially to suit the term, frequently referred to as 'night gowns' or 'bed gowns'. The sleeved waistcoat and night cap were as necessary for relaxed moments 'en famille' as the full skirted coat and periwig were for a social gathering.

Curiously enough this phase in our social history (roughly 1660–1800) is the only period when undress was a recognised variation from contemporary fashions, and the craze went so far as to lead to the introduction of a variety of fancy dress ensembles such as Pepys 'Indian Nightgown' and the long Persian gowns and turbans of the eighteenth century.

All manual work was carried out in undress—and towards the middle of the eighteenth century a sort of loose calf-length trouser became part of the working man's outfit in preference to the knee breeches with tiresome buttons and flaps. We first see these pictured by Watteau in his groups from the Commedia del Arte, and it is possible that the actor's 'fancy dress' had a definite effect on the fashions of the time. Early porcelain figurines and Wheatley's 'Cries of London' both illustrate these garments.

There is a definite connection between the romantic and pastoral ideal and the undress fashions of the sophisticate. The Shepherd and Shepherdess touch was not just a pictorial whimsey but an actual fashion. This is the fundamental clue to the eighteenth century modes and manners. To walk in Hyde Park, drink warm milk from a tethered cow, ape the tucked-up petticoats and floppy hat of the milk-maid—or if you were a man the loose cravat and un-dressed hair of her swain—was as elegant and daring as Marie Antoinette's pretty farming gestures at Versailles. How sincere it was with the youthful elegant is a matter of more serious debate, but the strictly sentimental attitude of the later eighteenth-century writers is undoubtedly a nostalgic gesture towards simplicity in spite of human viciousness. The artists, being realists, satirised this ideal into vulgarity.

Somewhere between satire and sentiment lies truth, and it seems almost impossible to find contemporary writings that are neither one thing nor the other. Certainly the make-up in the seventeenth and eighteenth centuries must have caused a great deal of comment. We read that patches were worn 'as many as spots on a leopards skin or freckles on the face of a Scotsman'. These, of course, might have been arranged to cover scars from smallpox, but, neverthe-less, it would be a strange habit to accustom oneself to. Again, in the early years of the eighteenth century, the French mode required that ladies' make-up should make them look unreal; with red cheeks, painted with lacquer.

It is only through the eyes of a contemporary audience that we can get these enlightening glimpses into the past. In my pursuit of such pictures I have found an incredible collection of brilliantly described characters. No modern explanation could compare with the shocked or amused entries of contemporary diarists or satirists. It therefore seems that the best method of approaching the subject is to quote largely from original sources, and to illustrate these descrip-tions with the nearest possible garments which still happily exist in many museums throughout the country, and to show just how they were worn.

For many years there has been a theory amongst those who make stage cos-tumes that period dress is incredibly complicated in cut and difficult to make. This misunderstanding is largely due to the effective work of the artist-designer, who is rightly more interested in colour and line than in the carrying out of his designs. If they have, vaguely, the right theatre effect, he is not particularly concerned how this is achieved.

I maintain that the whole problem should be reversed. If the original shape is used, the right effect will naturally be achieved. Make stays of the right shape, false hips or hoops, pad here or there as needed and the effect is immediately redolent of the period. Imagination can then have its fling.

Ordinary clothes have always been simple, for ordinary people had to make them by hand—no machines, no mass production, but economy and despatch must be pre-eminent factors in essential clothes.

From the accession of Charles II till the Regency a wider variety of characters are depicted on the stage than during any other period in history. Satirists were at work upon the frailties of human nature at the time of the Restoration to such an extent that one feels obliged to illustrate every kind of undress inferred or actually referred to in any of the famous productions. The types of character chosen were homely and sophisticated, prudes and professionals; each and every type glaringly demanded their own particular form of dress to distinguish them, theatrically, from each other. The eighteenth-century playwrights, if possible, drew an even stronger emphasis in their characters. It is, therefore, necessary to appreciate the subtle differences which can and do express so much distinction between the various types.

This difference is entirely due to the use of undress, and of outmoded fashions. The following article written in 1711 is as enlightening as anything could be to stress my case. Even without a knowledge of earlier fashions the points are clear.

'The Spectator. Vol. II

'July 28, 1711.   Fashions on circuit.

'One of the most fashionable women I met with in all the circuit was my landlady at Stains, where I chanced to be on holiday. Her commode was not half a foot high, and her petticoat within some yards of a modish circumference. In the same place I observed a young fellow with a tolerable periwig, had it not been covered with a hat that was shaped in the Ramilie-cock. As I proceeded on my journey, I observed the petticoat grow scantier and scantier, and about three score miles from London was so very unfashionable, that a woman might walk in it without any manner of inconvenience.

'Not far from Salisbury I took notice of a Justice of Peace's lady, who was at least ten years behind hand in her dress, but at the same time as fine as hands could make her. She was flounced and furbelowed from head to foot; every ribbon was wrinkled, and every part of her garments in curl, so that she looked

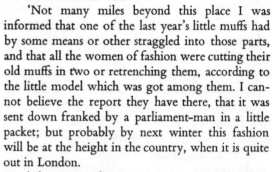

like one of those animals which in the country we call a Friezland hen.

'Not many miles beyond this place I was informed that one of the last year's little muffs had by some means or other straggled into those parts, and that all the women of fashion were cutting their old muffs in two or retrenching them, according to the little model which was got among them. I cannot believe the report they have there, that it was sent down franked by a parliament-man in a little packet; but probably by next winter this fashion will be at the height in the country, when it is quite out in London.

'The greatest beau at our next county sessions was dressed in a most monstrous flaxen periwig that was made in king William's reign. The wearer of it goes, it seems, in his own hair when he is at home, and lets his wig lie in buckle for a whole half year, that he may put it on upon occasion to meet the judges in it.

'I must not here omit an adventure which happened to us in a country church upon the frontiers of Cornwall. As we were in the midst of the service, a lady who is the chief woman of the place and had passed the winter at London with her husband, entered the congregation in a little head-dress and a hooped petticoat.

'Upon our way from hence we saw a young fellow riding towards us full gallop, with a bob wig and a black silken bag tied to it. . . . His stay was so very short, that we had only time to observe his new silk waistcoat, which was unbuttoned in several places to let us see that he had a clean shirt on, which was ruffled down to his middle.

'From this place, during our progress through the most western parts of the kingdom, we fancied ourselves in king Charles II reign, the people having made very little variations in their dress since that time. The smartest of the country squires appear still in the Monmouth-cock, and when they go a-wooing (whether they have any post in the militia or not) they generally put on a red coat. We were indeed, very much surprised, at the place we lay at last night, to meet with a gentleman who had accoutred himself in a night-cap-wig, a coat with long pockets and slit sleeves, and a pair of shoes with high scollop tops; but we soon found by his conversation that he was a person who laughed at the ignorance and rusticity of the country people, and was resolved to live and die in the mode.

'I will next year trouble you with such occurrences as I shall meet with in other parts of England. For I am informed there are greater curiosities in the northern circuit than in the western; and that a fashion makes its progress much slower into Cumberland than into Cornwall. I have heard in particular, that the Steenkirk arrived but two months ago at Newcastle, and that there are several commodes in those parts which are worth taking a journey thither to see.'

It is therefore of the greatest importance that any plays that are produced in or around this period should show striking contrasts in the styles of dress worn by the young and old, the fashionable or the sedate. One can quite safely use fashions twenty years apart, as long as it is remembered that only the bright young things, fops and ladies of fashion, wear the costumes of the year.

Having once learnt the essential contours and silhouette of the costume at any particular phase in its history, the next important item in costume design is the actual materials available at that time and the limitations imposed by methods of weaving, printing, dyeing, etc. It is surprising the amount of knowledge and skill that had been introduced into the textile trade as early as the seventeenth century. One is indeed hardly limited at all, except by the fact that the technique for producing floral patterns was limited to the use of one or two blocks. Therefore the gaudy modern floral is completely unsuitable, though a single coloured print can be quite useful. The simple woven pattern: spots, stripes, damasks, even plaids, would be more suitable than anything carrying a variety of colours. There seems to have been no limit to the knowledge of how to produce any possible colour for dyeing; but the mystery of the Oriental print, Indian, Persian or Chinese had not yet been solved.

Chapter I

1660–1680

IN 1660 we see a peculiar pageantry of men's styles, probably the most unmasculine of any period of history. John Evelyn's retrospective comments on the Coronation of Charles II commenced with the enlightening phrase, 'Clad in the fantastig habits of the time', and undoubtedly fantastic they were; though in all probability Molière and Samuel Pepys found nothing incongruous in them. Both in their way were willing to hold up to ridicule the styles of a decade earlier, or of a nation who showed less exuberance in their adoption of the Frenchman's frills and furbelows. They did, indeed, in Molière's own words, 'With readiness follow whatever changes custom introduces'.

Never have ribbon and lace been employed in such abundance. Not only were the coats and breeches decorated luxuriously with these two commodities, but every item of apparel could be 'laced', and this meant covered in lace. One of the most curious of contemporary fashions was that of wearing boot hose (fine linen stockings with a deep lace top, originally worn inside the boot, and referred to by Molière as rollers; see top of page), purely as a decoration, without any boots. These were tied just below the knee, with a garter, so that the lace top hung over, well down the calf, sometimes almost to the ankle. The ordinary silk or woollen hose were worn underneath these.

Pettitcoat breeches, another strange fashion, were so full that it was difficult to see they were not skirts. Normally knee-length, in some instances the under-breeches (a sort of baggy breeches) showed beneath the be-ribboned hem; this gave them a combination of warmth, and perhaps, decency. This fashion of showing the under-breeches is mentioned in 1663 by Pepys on May 10th when

FIG. 1

he put on 'a black cloth suit, with white lynings under all, as the fashion is to wear, to appear under the breeches' (see Fig. 1B). From a stage point of view these curious garments can be quite effective and comparatively easy to make. There is nothing particularly clever about their cut and materials are not heavy. One effect to be achieved is that of a hip-line rather than a waist-line; the decoration usually began on the hips, and to exaggerate this effect, the shirt was always worn very loose, and bloused out round the waist. Normally with the petticoat breeches a jackanapes coat, or little short one, was worn; these jackanapes coats had short sleeves, sometimes with a turned-back cuff at the elbow, sometimes with a more fancy arrangement and sometimes composed entirely of ribbons (see Figs. 1A and C). In their more sober interpretation, one can still see to-day their direct descendant in the short coat worn by the Swiss, Austrian and Bavarian countrymen. More extravagant and exotic designs were made entirely from lace and ribbon, split and cut in various places to show the elegance of the shirt beneath (see Fig. 1C).

Curiously enough, the most essential and most thought-of garment was the shirt; there are, indeed, still many of these beautifully made garments in existence. Made of the finest holland, which is what we would now call linen, and richly embroidered with insertions of lace, they were made to show. The absurd brevity of the jackanapes coat was designed on purpose to display embroidered or lace insertion down the front of the shirt and right down the sleeves from shoulder to wrist. The shirt was long, probably reaching below the calf of the leg when first put on, but the pantaloons or petticoat breeches, fitting tightly round the hips, hitched this up so that there were six or seven inches of loose shirt worn bloused round the waist. Lace ruffles were often sewn on at the wrist but another form of sleeve was quite straight with a wide opening at the wrist that could be held in at will with a wristband and lace frill which was detachable. This type of wide sleeve, with the wristband removed, is frequently seen in paintings of the 'sixties and 'seventies; when, following the tradition of the time, the arrangement of draperies was considered more artistically attractive than the actual fashion. Many of these shirts had neckbands with a lace collar attached, but before 1660 the collarband with bib front was introduced (see Fig. 2A); this was a band that went right round the throat and had two oblong pieces of embroidery or lace hanging down in the front only and tied with long cords or bands. When one sees the amazing prices of the hand-made lace of this time, it is obvious that fine underwear, which was always laced, was a very expensive part of the wardrobe. In all probability, many of

A   B

FIG. 2

the shirts that were made in the 'thirties or 'forties, were worn for a lifetime; the hand-made lace being almost indestructible.

Boot-hose were made in the same manner, with a deep lace border at the top; these served a functional purpose during the fashion for bucket-topped

4

boots, and they were not immediately cast aside when boots were no longer fashionable, being worn all through the 'sixties, gartered below the knee to give the impression of the boots which were no longer worn. It was not really until the appearance of the long coat that they were eventually discarded, and a trim leg in coloured stockings was considered the acme of elegance.

With Molière's delightful comedies to start our imaginations simmering, there could be no better foreground for the picture of life in the 1660's.

All the stupidities of fashion are set out here for our benefit, each item of apparel is called by its contemporary name and its use and misuse criticised. It is noticeable even at this early date that French fashions were ahead of English ones, and particularly in the wearing of powdered periwigs for men and patches for ladies; both of these fashions are remarked as new by Samuel Pepys several years later than they appear habitual to Molière.

In Molière's *The School for Husbands* Aristo's compliance with fashion rather than 'avoid obstinately what all the world pursues' stamps him as a reasonable human being. For then, as now, this is a safe course and one that is frequently found again and again on the stage, where contrast in clothes is so often one of the main features in the seventeenth- and eighteenth-century productions. This in itself is a point where knowledge of fashions is invaluable, the outmoded style is ridiculous in a few years, and therefore serves a dual purpose of emphasising a humorous character as well as giving a sharp contrast in shapes.

At certain periods in history an 'undress' or air of complete casualness in dress was considered a provocative and fashionable gesture, but this was not the case in 1660. Dress was quite definitely regarded as a social gesture of class consciousness, and the inability to conform to the dictates of fashion was considered as either a slovenly display of bad taste and non-conformity (with all the horror of non-conformity peculiar to that age), or else a necessary economy on the part of an inferior person.

To quote the description, no doubt satirical, of a young coxcomb, in Molière's words put into Sganarel's mouth . . .

'Oblige me to wear those little hats, which let their weak brains evaporate, and those powdered wigs, the vast business thereof obscures the figure of a human

5

countenance? Those short jerkins, but just below the arms and those large bands hanging down even to the navel? Those sleeves, which one sees dip in the sauce at table, and those petticoats called breeches? Those pretty shoes bedecked with ribbons, that make you look like rough-footed pigeons, and those large rollers,

Fig. 3

where, as in the stocks, the captive legs every morning are confined, and which make these accomplished gentlemen walk straddling, as if they were flying? . . .'

The long bands here referred to were the new hanging pieces from the collar (see Fig. 3A), and here we have the complete picture of the

6

fashionable man. In sharp contrast is the description of Sganarel's outmoded clothes . . .

'in spite of the fashions, I'll have a brim to my hat, under which my head may find a convenient shelter; a large long doubtlet, buttoned close as it ought to be, that it may keep the stomach warm to digest well; a pair of breeches made exactly to fit my thighs, and shoes wherein my feet may not be tortured; such as our forefathers wore—and whoever does not like me need only shut his eyes.'

Here we have two widely different costumes—Aristo's obviously that of 1660 and Sganarel's vaguely twenty or twenty-five years out of date, similar to the Quaker styles worn in the early years of the Commonwealth in England or by the Hollander of nonconformist principles in the 'forties.

'The Miser', first produced in 1668, also gives us descriptive evidence of two opposing styles, Harpagon upbraiding his son for extravagance, asks . . .

'To what purpose serve all these ribbons, with which you are so finely larded from head to foot; and whether half a dozen hooks and eyes would not be enough to fasten the knees of your breeches? What need is there to lay out money for perukes, when one may wear hair of one's own growth that costs nothing? I'll wager that what with perukes and what with ribbons there go at least twenty guineas.'

Another of Harpagon's enlightening references to fashionable dressing reads: 'Their three little bits of beard (see Fig. 3C) turned up like a cat's whiskers, their toupee wigs, their flowing breeches and their breasts open.' A later reference to his old-fashioned garb, shows that he too was wearing the fashions of the 'forties, 'She'll be charmed with your breeches tagged to your doublet with hooks and eyes,' for this shows that he was wearing a short doublet with tassets to it. We also find the only reference to a smock or overall. This comes in an enquiry from his two servants as to how they should dress for serving dinner with the question, 'Shall we throw off our canvas frocks, sir?'

The most accepted source of detailed costume reference in the 1660's is Samuel Pepys' Diary and, knowing the shape of clothes to which he refers from time to time, his comments become invaluable even if somewhat hackneyed. His frequent references to nightgowns, such as, 'Up, and in my nightgown, cap and neckcloth, undressed all day long', means, in reality, a dressing gown and nightcap (see illustration in tailpiece)—the sort worn when the wig was not in use. He refers in particular to his Indian nightgown, which might possibly have been a printed cotton, quilted, or merely a reference to its shape— the long, straight tunics or gowns worn with a sash. Again this reference to Indian does not necessarily mean that it came from India; the term covered practically all oriental imports. Fortunately there is still in existence a portrait of Pepys wearing such a garment, which he refers to as having hired particularly for the occasion (National Portrait Gallery).

In 1661 we find that he has first discarded the petticoat breeches '. . . this day left off half skirts and put on a waistcoate, my false tabby waistcoate with gold lace'. So one can safely assume that by October 1661, the long coat and waistcoat were already in vogue (see Fig. 4). This does not mean that the half-skirts, or petticoat breeches, were entirely discarded from that date; they prob-ably survived for at least another ten years and the plainer, undecorated sort, rather like loose football shorts, were worn by workmen in preference to the breeches for even longer. In 1665 he wears a new stuff suit with close knees '. . . which becomes me nobly as my wife says'. The first knee breeches (Fig. 2B).

Pepys' wardrobe can be taken to include all that a well-dressed man could possibly require. His scorn of others less well turned out is proof that there were many who cared less for their appearance. His extravagant dressing did in fact cause him many qualms, not only for the amount of money he spent on it but also for fear that he might be considered dishonest for so dressing. On May 1st, 1669,

> 'Up betimes. Called by my tailer, and there first put on a summer suit this year; but it was not my fine one of flowered tabby vest, and coloured camelott tunique, because it was too fine with the gold lace at the bands, that I was afraid to be seen in it; but put on the stuff suit I made the last year, which is now repaired . . . At noon home to dinner, and there find my wife extraordinary fine, with her flowered tabby gown that she made two years.ago, now laced exceeding pretty; and indeed was fine all over; and mighty earnest to go, though the day was very lowering; and she would have me put on my fine suit, which I did. And so anon we went alone through the town with our new liveries of serge, and the horses' manes and tails tied with red ribbons, and the standards gilt with varnish and all clean, and green reines, that people did mightily look

FIG. 4

upon us; and, the truth is, I did not see any coach more pretty, though more gay, than our's, all the day.'

It is from him that we learn the variety of materials used both for men's suits and women's gowns. At this period, apparently, there was no material used exclusively for either. He gives us a variety of etceteras such as the small things given to Valentines, green silk stockings, garters, shoe strings and jessamy gloves. He also mentions that green spectacles had already been invented and that long canes were very much in vogue.

Quite apart from his commentaries on his own wardrobe, he gives a lot of useful information on various economies exercised by his wife to refurbish her wardrobe. Almost any dress that was beginning to get shabby was covered with lace—'laced all over'—and a new petticoat worked wonders. He also tells us that false hair, not periwigs, was worn by women. On March 13th, 1665, '. . . my wife begun to wear light-coloured locks, quite white almost, which though it makes her look very pretty, yet not being natural, vexes me, that I will not have her wear them'. But in 1669 he seems to have got over his aversion or his wife has persuaded him otherwise, for they go together to visit Mrs. Grotier's, the Queen's tirewoman, for 'a pair of locks for my wife'. Quite probably she wore them two days later '. . . to Unthanke's where my wife dresses herself, having her gown this day laced, and a new petticoat; and so is indeed very fine'. He makes a very interesting announcement in the following month. 'My wife this day put on first her French gown, called a Sac, which becomes her very well, brought her over by W. Batelier.' This gown would not have been the pleated sac of the eighteenth century, but would probably be the original form of the gathered-back garment illustrated in so many of Watteau's paintings and later called a contouche.

Such references to habits of the time are invaluable. There is the curious description of men wearing their hats in church and how a Protestant preacher requires that these shall be removed; another entry of September 28th, 1662, reads: 'To the French Church at the Savoy, and there they have the Common Prayer Book read in French, and, which I never saw before, the minister do preach with his hat off, I suppose in further conformity with our Church.' We also find that swords were usually worn by footmen and that if you had been blooded you went out with your arm tied up in black ribbon, in much the same way as a red ribbon was worn after vaccination at a later date. Muffs were worn throughout the whole of this period—'This day I first did wear a muffe, being my wife's last year's muffe; and now I have bought her a new one, this serves me very well.' In 1663 he is enchanted with the latest fashions and riding habits of the ladies. . . .

'. . . By and by the King and Queene, who looked in this dress, a white laced waistcoate and a crimson short pettycoate, and her hair dressed à la négligence, mighty pretty: and the King rode hand in hand with her. Here was also my Lady Castlemaine, . . . She looked mighty out of humour, and had a yellow plume in her hat, which all took notice of, . . . I followed them up into White-hall, and into the Queene's presence, where all the ladies walked, talking and fiddling with their hats and feathers, and changing and trying one another's by one another's heads, and laughing. But it was the finest sight to me, con-sidering their great beautys and dress, that ever I did see in all my life. But, above all, Mrs. Stewart in this dresse, with her hat cocked and a red plume, with her sweet eye, little Roman nose, and excellent taille, is now the greatest beauty I ever saw, I think, in my life; and, if ever woman can, do exceed my Lady Castlemaine, at least in this dress: . . .'

The real structure of women's fashions depended entirely on the stays—the new look for the 'sixties was an extravagantly low point in front, and a curved line from heart to hip so that the bodice or waistcoat could be cut to curve out below the waist. This form was achieved with whalebone stiffened 'tassets' that splayed out from the waist. The stays were laced at the back and came down, in the back panel, almost to the bottom of the spine. (See Fig. 5.) The front panel was almost as long. Beneath the stays was worn the shift. This was rather like a nightdress (see Fig. 6); a long full garment of finest holland or lawn, sometimes with Cambric sleeves, either quite simple or very full and richly

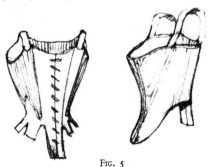

FIG. 5

adorned with lace and a gathered frill at the bottom of the sleeves and round
the neck. The frill at the neck-line was very low, but it could be pulled up above
the line of the stays to a decorous height should the wearer so desire. Many

FIG. 6

variations of this simple form were achieved. There was, for instance, the
use of a morning gown, one that did not require tight-fitting stays underneath,
but contained the necessary stiffening in the bodice itself. Separate sleeves

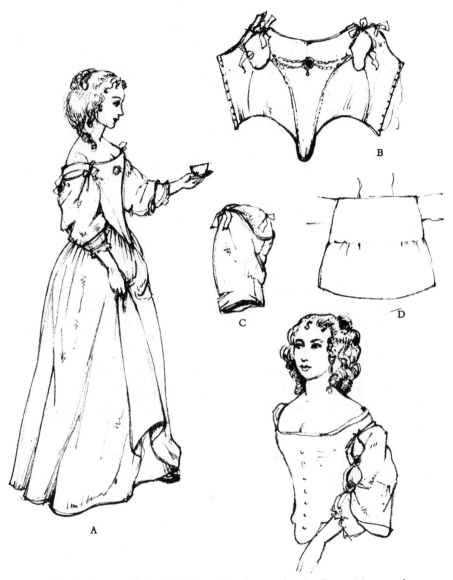

FIG. 7. Boned waistcoats with detachable sleeves. Details B, C and D taken from existing examples

(see Fig. 7) could be worn. The stiffening was contained in an embroidered and boned waistcoat or a coat with full, short sleeves. The boning of these garments was an art in itself, but the effect achieved was that of a very straight back, from shoulder to waist, and a slight curve out below the waist. So stiff were some of these coats or waistcoats, that if the head was bent forward the back resisted the curve of the body and stood away from the spine. (This silhouette is best seen in the Dutch paintings of the 'sixties.) The bone down the centre back was not worn much after 1680, although the straight back with curved waist continued until the hoops appeared in 1709 (see Figs. 8A and B).

The most obvious features of the gowns of 1660 to 1680 were those of the long trailing skirts behind and the extravagantly low neckline, off the shoulders in many instances, a fashion which, although it raised a storm of criticism and censorship in its own age even to the publication of a book in 1678 entitled *A Just and Reasonable Reprehension of Naked Breasts and Shoulders,* is a charming and useful one on the stage. The same book, incidentally, gives us the information that 'a monstrous superfluity of cloth or silk that must drag after them or be carried by another, or fardled behind them'; also, that the women were wearing periwigs at this date. One must, however, assume that this was not generally the case, though possibly a very useful fashion if the hair was not sufficiently luxurious to be managed. A curious phenomenon which I have noticed repeatedly in fashions, is that of hair-styles following the line and length of the skirt. This period is no exception. As the tied-back skirts of a gown form a sort of bustle and train, so the hair forms a knot with long curls behind; or as the skirts are bunched out at the side, so the hair is puffed and frizzed at the ears to give much the same effect. One can indeed find such cases in practically any period.

Cloaks, long gloves, high-heeled shoes with square, long toes, muffs, scarves, hoods, masks, fine linen and lace ruffles, tuckers and aprons, completed the normal outfit. Bonnets and caps and other head ornaments, apart from combs and geegaws, were not generally worn in England by the élite until the 'eighties; although the tiny lace bonnet with the bow in front first appeared in France in the late 'seventies, and coifs and bonnets were still worn by the elderly and old-fashioned. One thing to be borne in mind in the 1660's is that the extreme fashions were either French or Dutch. Charles II had come straight from the

FIG. 8

Parisian court of Louis XIV where frills and furbelows had been carried to excess, where each new peculiarity was exaggerated almost out of control; such as the great bunches and bows of ribbon worn on the shoes, the deep lace collar from shoulder to elbow (see Fig. 8) that practically pinioned a woman's arms to her sides and the long pointed stomacher which made the curtsy a movement from the knees only.

The Dutch fashions were neither so exaggerated nor so uncomfortable and we find pictures in abundance of the delightful little undress coats, full sleeved with minute pin-tucks and with a flared basque often trimmed with fur.

One of the most interesting economies of the 1660's can be noticed in these same Dutch paintings. One light coloured gown, with silver lace decoration round the bottom and up the front of the petticoat, can be changed to appear as three separate ensembles. This is particularly noticeable in paintings by Terborch. In the first instance we see the gown with a white top, off the shoulders and very *décolleté* in cut, with slightly puffed ribboned sleeves and a neatly fitting basque. In the next painting, a blue velvet bodice is worn with the same petticoat, not quite so *décolleté* and with fuller sleeves. The third transformation is a black velvet gown with a trailing skirt split at the front to show the same lace petticoat beneath and a deep transparent lace collar veiling the shoulders from neck to elbow (see Fig. 8). Such variety would give the designer both characteristic forms and economy in material for the same play. Even the change of a collar at this time could make formal dress into something more like a morning gown. There is no doubt that, with materials as expensive as they were in the seventeenth century, such economies were a perfectly accepted mode of transformation. In another of the Dutch paintings we see a child with a blue tight-fitting bodice, a striped pink and blue underpetticoat and a pink tucked-up petticoat, apparently attached to the blue bodice. Obviously at this time, the petticoat and bodice were separate and it was not until the 'eighties or even 'nineties that the all-in-one gown, traditionally attributed to the eighteenth century, came into its own.

There is an interesting similarity in the shape of the hairdressing, male and female, which occurs almost without exception throughout the whole of this period. Once one has established whether heads should be round or square,

FIG. 9.   1660–1670

puffed, padded or apparently close-cropped, one has to a reasonable extent achieved the general aspect of the head shape of any particular period. In 1660 and sometimes as late as 1665 one finds that the style in women's hairdressing revolved chiefly round the careful arrangement of the little forehead curls, the parting which ran right round the forehead, the hair drawn flat on the top of the head, in some instances resembling a tight-fitting velvet cap, and curls falling more or less naturally down to the shoulders. A personal whim decided whether this hair style should be decorated with pearls or a comb at the back, and obviously the natural differences of the hair itself, straight, curly or iron waved, gave a certain amount of scope and variety. However, almost as soon as Katherine of Braganza arrived in England, although her Portuguese hair styles caused King Charles to say that they had brought him a bat instead of a woman, the form of the hairdressing altered perceptibly and the bat-eared effect became general. When Lely painted Lady Castlemaine in 1662, her hair was quite definitely puffed and padded out over the ears, although the same arrangement of curls on the forehead, and curls brushing the shoulders, still persisted (see Fig. 9).

Throughout the 'sixties the fashionable and unfashionable could be easily separated by the width of the hair style. Before 1670 the men's periwigs also followed the same line, flat on top and very wide from ear to shoulder. Lely's delightful little painting of the child Lady Elizabeth Percy, done in 1665, gives one an excellent idea of how the hair was trained to the fashionable effect. Here we see how it was brushed back from the temples over a lace cap, with the curls arranged at the back of the head and apparently pinned on to the cap at the back. (See top centre, Fig. 9.) By 1670 a centre parting had become universal, and the puffing out began from the top of the head and not the ear. Such puffing apparently was dependent on the amount of hair one had to play with. In certain pictures it is quite evident that the hair was little more than shoulder length; in which case one or two side curls touched the shoulders and the rest was absorbed in the mass of curls over the ears. Children at this time wore a little flat lace cap on the top of their head, with a bow of ribbon at either side, the ribbons adding to the fashionable contour and the cap holding the hair flat on the top of the head. (See bottom, Fig. 10.)

There is hardly any other phase in fashion history—with the exception

18

FIG. 10.   1670–1680

of the present century—when bonnets or caps of some sort or another were not worn by a very large section of female society.

It is therefore doubly important to know the hairdressing styles which can be associated with the 1660's and 1670's.

Perhaps a source of real inspiration can be traced to the fashionable interest in the 'Classic' tradition at this time.

The term 'Classic' was used widely—as indeed was the term 'Indian'. But there is nevertheless an unmistakable suggestion in the contemporary hair styles that they were inspired by some of the late Roman ladies' heads which can be examined in the British Museum today.

When riding dress was worn ladies wore periwigs and hats similar in style to those of their male escorts—this fashion persisted well into the eighteenth century.

At other times the hair was so puffed and padded by the addition of false curls and switches that a hood or lace scarf over the head was far easier to wear than a hat, and probably much more comfortable.

Another hair style, about 1675, said to have evolved from Madame Fontange tying up unruly curls with a garter, first brought the top-knot or bow of ribbon directly over the brow into general use. This bunch of curls eventually developed into the strange horned effect, which was achieved by plastering with pomade, apparently like a stiff setting lotion, so that the shorter curls on the forehead could be forced into standing up. The introduction of the bonnet was probably contemporary, as the frontal frills obviously gave one something to pin the curls on to. In the early days of the Fontange or top-knot, a tight-fitting little lace bonnet was frequently worn on the back of the head with just a bow of ribbon in the front; and naturally the wide puffing at the sides of the hair disappeared and the curls were tied back in a cluster at the back of the neck.

Chapter II

1680—1700

THE scene changed in the mid-'eighties to a more stylised silhouette. This was not entirely due to court changes at the coming of Dutch William, but was a certain culmination of sophisticated ideas from a variety of countries. The most tangible of these ideas was the introduction of fashion drawings. These plates were drawn in Paris by an artist by the name of J. O. de St. Jean, and apparently had as startling an effect on the dress of the times as Dior's New Look in 1948. The earliest dated one is 1686 and they clearly show the cut and make of both men and women's fashion. These naturally established a formality in dress which had not previously occurred. Here we can see the full skirted coat (see Figs. 4 and 11) in its earliest form, with the flare of the skirts commencing well below the hips, large pockets used as decoration, the long knee-length waistcoat with buttons all down the front and sleeves split at the wrist to turn back over the deep cuff of the coat, sashes and sword belts, muffs, rolled stockings, high-heeled buckled shoes, laced cravats and long curly wigs, and, for the fop, masses of ribbons—ribbons at the throat, bunches of ribbons on the shoulders, ribbons decorating the hilt of the sword and ribbon garters; large beaver hats, with a wide hard brim, were worn turned up at the side or the front or with the brim rolled and decorated with a feather as pleased the wearer.

The pockets were first of all decorated upright slits in the front of the skirts, then the flap pocket was worn very near the hem so that there was literally only space for the pocket itself at the bottom of the coat. Handkerchiefs were a new and elegant item and were worn so that they showed hanging from

21

.FIG. 11

the pocket opening. This fashion, oddly enough, persisted in spite of pick-pockets for many years. Such coats were made from a variety of materials, and trimmed with an extravagance of decoration still reminiscent of the early days of the Restoration. Embroidery on men's coats had not, as yet, come in. Lace, tassels, fur, fringe, silver and gold cord and 'galloon' vied with coloured ribbons, buttons and loops, frogging and a dozen other fashionable fripperies. There were even instances of embossed leather decoration, and a buckskin coat for riding or hard wear could carry an embossed design round hem and front. The sword-belt, the sash and the muff all added to the general splendour of the outfit.

Congreve supplies us with the essentials of the male silhouette in 1692 in his *Love for Love*.

'Long wigs, laced coats, Steinkirk cravats . . .' and Farquahar adds such assorted extras as 'Slabbering bib', 'Your Starched band, set by mode and figure', 'A new Burgundy for my brother's head'.

All these items are easily traceable to the 'nineties, the Steinkirk cravat after the battle of Steinkirk, 1692. The 'slabbering bib' was yet another offensive term for the spread-out cravat. 'The starched band', a stiffened cravat with long ends. Tying the cravat was a feat of some skill. 'She who can tie with quaintest art the spruce cravat string, wins his heart.' The Steinkirk cravat was supposedly invented on the field of battle as a more sensible fashion than the carefully tied laced cravat. The ways in which the latter could be tied varied considerably and some of the drawings and sculpture of the time show a studied nonchalance of twists that defy verbal explanation. (See Fig. 12.) Grinling Gibbons has left us a wonderful lime wood carving of the more formal arrangement of the tied cravat in the 'eighties, a pure essay on the design of light and shade that could occur in lace (see Fig. 13). This is on exhibition at the Victoria and Albert Museum. All these cravats were edged with lace from 9 to 12 inches deep, according to the way they were to be tied. We do not find the plainer forms until the vast periwigs begin to be replaced by the small white wig.

At this time the periwig was in its most exaggerated form. Congreve's 'Long wigs' was putting it quite mildly, for they were competing with the head-dress of the ladies and gradually climbing up higher in the front—and frequently forming two great curls like question-marks over the foreheads. These curls were often referred to as 'horns' and the contemporary reference is frequently employed in its ruder sense. There was an abundance of curls

FIG. 12.   Steinkirk cravat

FIG. 13

and some of the periwigs were so long that they almost reached the waist (see tail piece). After this particular fashion had become as exaggerated as was humanly bearable came the introduction of the full-bottomed wig, a style which had obviously given up the unequal struggle to compete with the effect of real human hair, and was divided into three large tangled masses separated so that the shoulders could have reasonable movement. The full-bottomed wig remained in fashion for older men and for the legal profession well into the 'forties of the next century; contrasting strangely with the tight-fitting white wigs which were generally worn. Gold filings were sometimes sprinkled over the curls, so that they might glint in the sunlight or candlelight. Scented hair powder was fairly general and the use of sweet-scented 'Pulvillio' was as popular as the use of scented and fringed gloves. The latter were often referred to as 'Oranges' because of their orange blossom perfume. No form of personal adornment was deemed too extravagant to have its adherents.

By 1695 the coat typical of the eighteenth century had achieved its standardised form to vary comparatively little for nearly a century (see Fig. 14).

Coloured stockings with a great padded roll at the knee were, according to contemporary legend, introduced so that in kneeling there should be some protection to the knees of the devout. They were referred to as 'rolls' and were undoubtedly exaggerated in size by the fashionable man-about-town. Pearl-coloured hose, as well as those shot with silver, were considered even more refined than those embroidered with clocks in various colours, and a plain coloured stocking was worn for more everyday affairs.

The shoes were rather long and narrow, with a squared toe and high, clumsy red heels. The tongue, or flap, that came up the instep was exaggerated and often scalloped at the top and rolled down to show a scarlet lining. Buckles were of vast proportions and bought separately from the shoes to fasten to one side of the instep strap and secure both sides. Once in favour and fashion, buckles were worn for over a century.

There is a mixture of language in the fashionable terms, particularly in men's clothes. The Brandenburg or morning gown, something like a short dressing gown, is obviously German, and probably filtered into our vocabulary through William and Mary; 'picards', the fashionable name for shoes; 'che-dreux', the periwig, and a dozen other such terms all have their European origin. It was indeed more fashionable to pretend not to be English than to pride oneself on the age and nobility of one's family. This habit persists almost throughout the eighteenth century, and it is not until the closing years of that

FIG. 14

century and the beginning of the nineteenth when this country was isolated in the Napoleonic wars, that John Bull pride once more became an irritation to all foreigners.

For the less exotic, the merchant or city man, there were obviously a hundred economies that could be exercised. Ned Ward described a few of the more obvious tradesmen and businessmen to be seen in London before 1700. The following four paragraphs give us useful information.

' "Did you take notice of the gentleman in blue coat, red stockings, silver-hilted sword, and edged hat, who sat at the upper end of the table?" . . . "There was a handsome young fellow who sat next him, with a full periwig on, and a whole piece of muslin about his neck, who stank as strong of orange-flower water as a Spaniard does of garlic." '

'He entered the tavern first, like a young squire attended with his father's chaplain, for a black coat and band are as great signs of a parson or pedagogue as a blue frok is of a butcher or a tallow-chandler.'

' "He that sat near him, in the plate-buttoned suit and white beaver hat, is a kind of amphibious rascal, a compound of two sorts of villiany." '

' "What are these eagle-faced fellows, in their narrow-brimmed white beavers, jacket-coats, a spur on one heel, and bended sticks in their hands . . ." "Those blades are a sort of Smithfield fox called horse dealers." '

The white hat seems to have appeared some time during the 'nineties and was adopted again by Beau Nash in the following century. In these early references the inference is apparently far from fashionable, and seems to carry a stigma of some sort.

It is probably the alteration in the design of materials that gave this era its particular sophistication. There is something incredibly architectural in the whole form. The petticoat that had been laced or trimmed with galloon was now fringed, corded and quilted (see Figs. 15 and 18B). Designs rich with gold or silver thread followed the same curvilinear form as ironwork. The material of a gown was frequently printed with some fine all-over pattern, or a woven

27

A

C

B

FIG. 15

stripe introduced. The stays were straighter in the front, allowing no curve to be visible between breasts and hip bone (see Fig. 16). This form of tight lacing gave a pouter pigeon effect, and exaggerated the backward curve in the spine so that there was a definite tendency towards the bustle. One sees the fashion plates exaggerating the fashionable stance—elbows well back, muff over the stomach, the face well-powdered with patches, or a mask or half-mask held in front of the face. As Congreve remarks in *The Way of the World*, 'Fans spread and streamers out', and the picture is before you.

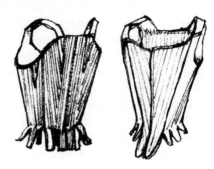

FIG. 16

The most noticeable feature of women's costume was the new interest in head tiring. The frivolous arrangement of frills worn on top of the head quickly turned into a series of lace erections held in place by wire, starch, pins and stiffened ribbons, eventually attached to a bonnet. Each item of this head ornament was given a French term. An amusing defence of these French terms was published in 1690 in *Mundus Propensus*; saying in delightfully modern manner—'would men suggest that the Lady said to her maid "Pass me that thing to wear on my thing—no, not that thing, the other thing"?'—surely the best possible reason for introducing French terms? By this alone, one appreciates the fact that the tall head-dress called a commode, or pinner, was not Dutch and did not originally come from Holland with William and Mary. Because of this erection on the head the female silhouette had changed radically. Various contemporary writers began to satirise this latest feminine folly and eventually called forth from John Evelyn's daughter a witty though elongated rhyming warning to young men about to marry, on the absurdities of female attire, and the extravagant demands they must expect. This poem is so unusual and amusing that I have included it in the following pages—it gives, far better than any other known contemporary work, not only the fashion in clothes, jewellery, head-dresses, lace and linen, but a great deal of the habits of the time. According to Evelyn's diary, this was written by Mary Evelyn in 1684, although it was not

29

published until five years after her death, which occurred in 1685, and it then appeared under her father's name and not hers, entitled *A Voyage to Maryland*.

This definitely gives us a date for the head-dress only a year after the death of Charles II, and also refers to gloves trimmed and laced as fine as 'Nell's', meaning, of course, Nell Gwynn. All these amazing aids to beauty are entered in the 'Dictionary' at the back of this little book, and those who are interested can find all the contemporary expressions for every frill and curl—for each and every one had a fashionable name which probably changed as fast as the fashions did themselves.

No further explanation of these fantastic female fashions, except the accompanying drawings, are necessary.

It was between the years 1699 and 1702 that the commode climbed up to its most exaggerated height; the fashion had spread to all sections of the public and eventually was so ridiculous that the wildest flights of fancy towards the skies were indulged in only by women of infamous character and those determined to attract attention.

Again Ned Ward pointed his finger mockingly at these fashions:

'. . . the wenches in their morning gowns and wadded waistcoats (see Figs. 17 and 19), without stays, began to flow fast into the walks. One with slip shoes, without stockings, and a dirty smock (visible through a crepe petticoat) was stepping from the ale-house to her lodgings, with a parcel of pipes in one hand, and a gallon pot of guzzle in the other, yet her head was dressed up to as much advantage, as if the members of her body were sacrificed to all wickedness, to keep her ill-looking face in a little finery.

'. . . As we stumbled along my friend bid me notice a shop wherein sat three or four very provoking damsels, with as much velvet on their backs as would have made a burying-pall for a country parish, or a holiday coat for a physician, being glorified at bottom with gold fringes, so that I thought at first they might be parsons' daughters who had borrowed their fathers' pulpit clothes to use as scarves to go visiting in. Each has as many patches as are spots in a leopard's skin or freckles in the face of a Scotsman.

'By help of paint, powder and patches, they were of a wax-work complexion, and thus dressed: their under-petticoats were white dimity, embroidered like a turkey-work chair, or a fool's doublet, with red, green, blue and yellow; their pin-up coats of Scotch plaid, adorned with bugle lace; and their gowns of

30

FIG. 17. Details of 'wadded waistcoats'

printed calico. But their heads were dressed up to the best advantage, like a vintner's bar-keeper or a churchwarden's daughter upon an Easter Sunday.'

Not only do we catch the inference of the stigma that was beginning to be attached to this head-dressing, but we can also see enlightening glimpses of

A

B

FIG. 18. Sultane and surtout

'undress' in the 'wadded waistcoats' and 'no stays'. We are also shown the colour-ful pageantry of embroideries, plaids and printed calicoes that typify the years immediately preceding the reign of Queen Anne.

A

VOYAGE TO MARYLAND;

OR, THE

LADIES' DRESSING-ROOM.

Negotii sibi qui volet vim parare,
   navim et mulierem, haec duo comparato.
nam nullae magis res duae plus negotii
habent, forte si occeperis exornare.
neque unquam satis hae duae res ornantur.
neque eis ulla ornandi satis satietas est.
                Plaut. Poenulus. Act. I. Scen 2.

Whoever has a mind to abundance of trouble,
   Let him furnish himself with a Ship and a
      Woman.
For no two things will find you more Employment
If once you begin to rig them out with all their
      Streamers,
Nor are they ever sufficiently adorned,
Or satisfy'd that you have done enough to
      set them forth.

He that will needs to *Marry-Land*
   Adventure, first must understand
For's Bark what Tackle to prepare,
'Gainst Wind and Weather, wear and tare.
Of Point *d'Espagne* a rich *Cornet*,
Two *Night-Rails*, and a *Scarf* beset
With a great Lace, a *Colleret*.

33

One black Gown of Rich Silk, which odd is
Without one Colour'd, Embroider'd Bodice:
Four Petticoats for Page to hold up,
Four short ones nearer to the Crup:
Three *Manteaus*, nor can Madam less
Provision have for due undress;
Nor *demy Sultane, Spagnolet,*
Nor Fringe to sweep the Mall forget:
Of under Bodice three neat pair
Embroider'd, and of Shoosas fair:
Short under Petticoats pure fine,
Some of *Japan* Stuff, some of *Chine,*
With Knee-high Galoon bottomed,
Another quilted White and Red;
With a broad *Flanders* Lace below:
Four pair of *Bas de soy* shot through
With Silver. Diamond Buckles too.
For Garters, and as Rich for Shoo.
Twice twelve day Smocks of *Holland* fine,
With *Cambric* Sleeves, rich Point to joyn,
(For she despises *Colbertine*).
Twelve more for night, all *Flanders* lac'd,
Or else she'll think her self disgrac'd:
The same her Night-Gown must adorn,
With Two Point Wastcoats for the Morn:
Of Pocket *Mouchoirs* Nose to drain,
A dozen lac'd, a dozen plain:
Three Night-Gowns of rich *Indian* Stuff,
Four Cushion-Cloths are scarce enough,
Of Point, and *Flanders,* nor forget
Slippers embroidered on Velvet:
A *Manteau* Girdle, Ruby Buckle,
And Brilliant Diamond Rings for Knuckle:
Fans painted, and perfumed three;
Three Muffs of *Sable, Ermine, Grey*;
Nor reckon it among the Baubles,
A *Palatine* also of *Sables.*

34

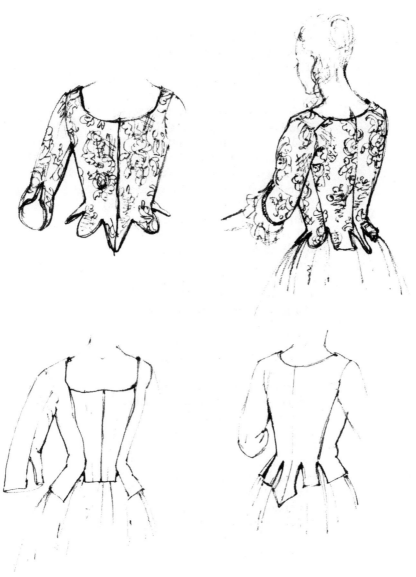

FIG. 19.   Sleeved waistcoats, 1670–1700

A Saphire Bodkin for the Hair,
Or sparkling Facet Diamond there:
Then *Turquois, Ruby, Emerauld* Rings
For Fingers, and such pretty things;
As Diamond Pendants for the Ears,
Must needs be had, or two Pearl Pears,
Pearl Neck-lace, large and Oriental,
And Diamond, and of Amber pale;
For Oranges bears every Bush,
Nor values she cheap things a rush.
Then Bracelets for her Wrists bespeak,
(Unless her Heart-strings you will break)
With Diamond *Croche* for Breast and Bum,
Till to hang more on there's no room.
Besides these Jewels you must get
Cuff Buckles and an handsom Set
Of Tags for Palatine, a curious Hasp
The Manteau 'bout her Neck to clasp:
Nor may she want a Ruby Locket,
Nor the fine sweet quilted Pocket;
To play at *Ombre*, or *Basset*,
She a rich *Pulvil* Purse must get,
With Guineas fill'd, on Cards to lay,
Nor is she troubled at ill fortune,
For should the bank be so importune,
To rob her of her glittering Store,
The amorous Fop will furnish more.
Pensive and mute, behind her shoulder
He stands, till by her loss grown bolder,
Into her lap *Rouleau* conveys,
The softest thing a Lover says:
She grasps it in her greedy hands,
Then best his Passion understands;
When tedious languishing has fail'd,
Rouleau has constantly prevail'd.
But to go on where we left off,
Though you may think what's said enough;

36

This is not half that does belong
To the fantastick Female Throng:
In Pin-up Ruffles now she flaunts,
About her Sleeves are *Engageants*:
Of Ribbon, various *Echelles*
Gloves trimm'd, and lac'd as fine as *Nell's.*
Twelve dozen *Martial*, whole, and half,
Of *Jonquil, Tuberose*, (don't laugh)
Frangipan, Orange, Violett,
Narcissus, Jassemin, Ambrett.
And some of *Chicken* skin for night,
To keep her Hands plump, soft, and white:
Mouches for pushes, to be sure,
From *Paris* the *tré-fine* procure,
And *Spanish* Paper, Lip, and Cheek,
With Spittle sweetly to belick:
Nor therefore spare in the next place,
The Pocket *Sprunking* Looking-Glass;
Calembuc Combs in *Pulvil* case,
To set, and trim the Hair and Face:
And that the Cheeks may both agree,
Plumpers to fill the Cavity.
The *Settée, Cupée* place aright,
Frelange, Fontange, Favorite;
Monte la haut, and *Palisade*,
Sorti, Flandan (great helps to Trade)
Burgoigne, Jardiné, Cornett,
Frilal next upper Pinner set,
Round which it does our Ladies please
To spread the Hood call'd *Rayonnes:*
Behind the Noddle every Baggage
Wears bundle *Choux*, in *English* Cabbage.
Nor *Cruches* she, nor *Confidents*,
Nor *Passagers* nor *Bergers* wants;
And when this Grace Nature denies,
An Artificial *Tour* supplies;
All which with *Meurtriers* unite,

37

And *Creve-Coeurs* silly Fops to smite,
Or take in Toil at *Park* or *Play*,
Nor Holy *Church* is safe, they say,
Where decent Veil was wont to hide
The modest Sex Religious Pride:
Lest these yet prove too great a Load,
'Tis all comprised in the *Commode*;
Pins tipt with Diamond Point, and head,
By which the Curls are fastened,
In radiant *Firmament* set out,
And over all the Hood *sur-tout*:
This Face that *E'rst* near head was plac'd
Imagine now about the Wast,
For *Tour* on *Tour*, and *Tire* on *Tire*,
Like Steeple Bow, or *Grantham* Spire,
Or *Septizonium* once at *Rome*,
(But does not half so well become
Fair Ladies Head) you there behold
Beauty by Tyrant Mode controll'd.
The graceful *Oval*, and the *Round*,
This *Horse* Tire does quite confound.
And Ears like *Satyr*, Large and Raw,
And bony Face, and hollow Jaw;
This monstrous Dress does now reveal
Which well plac'd Curles did once conceal.
Besides all these, 'tis always meant
You furnish her Appartment,
With *Moreclack* Tapistry, Damask Bed,
Or Velvet richly embroidered:
Branches, *Brasero*, *Cassolets*,
A *Cofre-fort*, and Cabinets,
Vasas of Silver, *Porcelan*, store
To set, and range about the Floor:
The Chimney Furniture of Plate,
(For Iron's now quite out of date:)
Tea-Table, *Skreens*, Trunks, and Stand,
Large Looking-Glass richly *Japan'd*,

An hanging Shelf, to which belongs
Romances, Plays, and Amorous Songs;
Repeating Clocks, the hour to show
When to the Play 'tis time to go,
In Pompous Coach, or else Sedan'd
With Equipage along the *Strand*,
And with her new *Beau* Foppling mann'd.
A new Scene to us next presents,
The Dressing-Room, and Implements,
Of Toilet Plate Gilt, and Emboss'd,
And several other things of Cost:
The Table Miroir, one Glue Pot,
One for Pomatum, and what not?
Of *Washes, Unguents*, and *Cosmeticks*,
A pair of Silver Candlesticks;
Snuffers, and Snuff-dish, Boxes more,
For Powders, Patches, Waters store,
In silver Flasks, or Bottles, Cups
Cover'd, or open, to wash Chaps;
Nor may *Hungarian* Queen's be wanting,
Nor store of Spirits against fainting:
Of other waters rich and sweet,
To sprinkle Handkerchief is meet;
D'Ange, Orange, Mill-Fleur, Myrtle,
Whole Quarts the Chamber to bequirtle:
Of Essence *rare, & le meilleure*
From *Rome*, from *Florence, Montpellier*,
In *Filgran Casset* to repel,
When Scent of *Gousset* does rebel,
Though powder'd *Allom* be as good
Well strew'd on, and well understood;
For Vapours that offend the Lass,
Of Sal-*armoniack* a Glass:
Nor Brush for Gown, nor Oval Salver
Nor Pincushion, nor Box of Silver,
Baskets of *Fil' gran*, long and round,
Or if *Japonian* to be found,

And the whole Town so many yield,
Calembuc Combs by dozens fill'd
You must present, and a world more,
She's a poor Miss can count her store.
The Working Apron too from *France*,
With all its trim Apurtenance;
Loo Masks, and whole, as Wind do blow,
And Miss abroad's dispos'd to go:
Hoods by whole dozens, White and Black,
And store of Coiffs she must not lack,
Nor Velvet Scarfs about her Back,
To keep her warm; all these at least
In *Amber'd* Skins, or quilted Chest
Richly perfum'd, she Lays, and rare
Powders for Garments, some for Hair
Of *Cyprus*, and of *Corduba*,
And the Rich *Polvil* of *Goa*:
Nor here omit the Bob of Gold
Which a *Pomander* Ball does hold,
This to her side she does attach
With Gold *Crochet*, or *French Pennache*.
More useful far than *Ferula*.
For any saucy Coxcomb's Jaw:
A graceful Swing to this belongs,
Which he returns in Cringe, and Songs,
And languishings to kiss the hand,
That can Perfumed blows command.
All these, and more in order set,
A large rich Cloth of Gold *Toilet*
Does cover, and to put up Rags,
Two high Embroider'd Sweet Bags,
Or a large Perfum'd *Spanish* Skin,
To wrap up all these Trinkets in.
But I had almost quite forgot,
A *Tea* and *Chocolate* Pot,
With *Molionet*, and Caudle Cup,
Restoring Breakfast to sup up:

Porcelan Saucers, Spoons of Gold,
Dishes that refin'd Sugars hold;
Pastillios de Bocca we
In Box of beaten Gold do see.
Inchas'd with Diamonds, and *Tweeze*
As Rich and Costly as all these,
To which a bunch of *Onyxes,*
And many a Golden Seal there dangles,
Mysterious Cyphers and new fangles,
Gold is her Toothpick, Gold her Watch is,
And Gold is every thing she touches
But tir'd with numbers I give o're.
Arithmetick can add no more,
Thus Rigg'd the Vessel, and Equipp'd
She is for all Adventures Shipp'd,
And Portion e're the year goes round,
Does with her Vanity confound.

THE

FOP-DICTIONARY.

OR AN

Alphabetical Catalogue of the hard and foreign Names, and Terms of the Art COSMETICK, &c. together with their Interpretations, for Instruction of the Unlearned.

Attache.

Any thing which fastens to another, &c.

Bas de soye shot through.

Silk Stockings with Gold, or Silver thread wove into the Clock.

Berger.

A plain small Lock (a la Shepherdesse) turn'd up with a Puff.

Bourgoigne.

The first part of the Dress for the Head next the Hair.

FIG. 20

Branches.

Hanging Candlesticks, like those used in Churches.

Brasiere.

A large Vessel or moving-Hearth of Silver for Coals transportable into any Room, much used in Spain.

Calumbuc.

A certain precious Wood, of an agreeable Scent, brought from the Indies.

Campaine.

A kind of narrow picked Lace.

Casset.

A Dressing Box.

Cassolet.

Perfuming Pot or Censer.

Choux.

The great round Boss or Bundle, resembling a Cabbage, from whence the French give it that name.

Cofre-fort.

A strong Box of some precious or hard wood, &c. bound with gilded Ribs.

Colbertine.

A Lace resembling Net-Work of the Fabrick of Mons'eur Colbert, Superintendent of the French Kings Manufactures.

Collaret.

A sort of Gorget.

Commode.

A frame of Wire, cover'd with Silk, on which the whole Head-Attire is adjusted at once upon a Bust, or property of Wood carved to the Breasts, like that which Perruque-makers set upon their Stalls.

Confidants.

Smaller Curles near the Ears.

Cornet.

The upper Pinner, dangling about the Cheeks, like Hounds Ears.

Cosmeticks.

Here used for any Effeminate Ornament, also artificial Complections and Perfumes.

Creve-coeur.

Heart-breakers, the two small curl'd Locks at the Nape of the Neck.

Crochet.

The Hook to which are chain'd the Ladies Watch, Seals, and other Intaglias, &c.

Cruches.

Certain smaller Curles, placed on the Forehead.

Cuppee.

A kind of Pinner.

Echelles.

A Pectoral, or Stomacher lac'd with Ribbon, like the rounds of a Ladder. (See Figs. 15A, 20C and 22B.

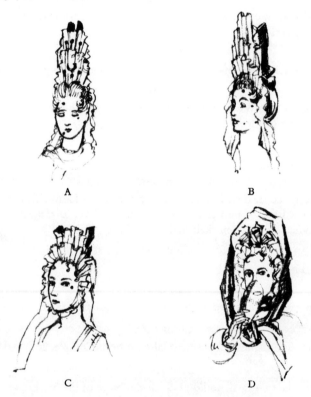

A

B

C

D

Fig. 21. The three top illustrations show various ways in which the 'Frelan', 'Flandan' or 'Settee' could be arranged. These are constructed from a bonnet with streamers, the frills and ribbons attached afterwards with the help of pins and wire. The bottom drawing shows the hood and mask for outdoor wear.

44

Engageants.
Deep double Ruffles, hanging down to the Wrists.

Favorites.
Locks dangling on the Temples.

Ferula.
An Instrument of Wood us'd for Correction of lighter faults, more sensibly known to School-Boys than to Ladies.

Fil-grain'd.
Dressing-Boxes, Baskets or whatever else is made of Silver Wire-work.

Flandan.
A kind of Pinner joyning with the Bonnet.

Firmament.
Diamonds, or other precious Stones heading the Pins which they stick in the Tour, and Hair, like Stars.

Frelan.
Bonnet and Pinner together.

Font-Ange.
The Top-knot so call'd from Mademoiselle de Fontange, one of the French King's Mistresses who first wore it.

Gris.
The Grey Furr of Squirrels bellies.

Japonian.
Anything Varnished with Laccar or China Polishing, or that is old or fantastical.

Jardinee.
That single Pinner next the Bourgogne.

Loo Maske.
An half Mask.

Martial.
The Name of a famous French Perfumer, emulating the Frangipani of Rome.

Miroir.

In general, any Looking-Glass; but here, for the Table, Toilet or Pocket Sprunking-Glass.

Molionet.

The Instrument us'd to mingle Chocolate with the Water.

Monte la haut.

Certain degrees of Wire to raise the Dress.   (Head-dress)

Mouchoire.

It was Rude, Vulgar, and Uncourtly to call it Handkerchief.

Mouches.

Flies, or, Black Patches, by the Vulgar.

Meurtrieres.

Murderers; a certain Knot in the Hair, which ties and unites the Curls.

Palatine.

Formerly call'd Sables, or Tippet, because made of the Tails of that Animal.

Palisade.

A Wire sustaining the Hair next to the Dutchess, or first Knot.

Passagere.

A Curl'd Lock next the Temples.

Pastillo di Bocca.

Perfum'd Lozenges to improve the Breath.

Pennache.

Any Bunch or Tassel of small Ribbon.

Plumpers.

Certain very thin, round, and light Balls, to plump out, and fill up the Cavities of the Cheeks, much us'd by old Court-Countesses.

Pulvil.

The Portugal term for the most exquisite Powders.

Raggs.

A Compendious Name generally us'd for all sorts of Point, Lace, &c. whence the Women who bring them to Ladies Chambers are call'd Ragg-Women; but whilst in their Shops, Exchange-Women.

Rare, le meilleures.

Best, and most Excellent; but in Language de beau rare & le meilleure, happily rhyming with Montpellier.

A   FIG. 22   B.

Rayonne.

Upper Hood, pinn'd in Circle, like the Sunbeams. (See Fig. 22A.)

Rouleau.

Is Forty Nine Guineas, made up in a Paper Roll, which Monsieur F—— Sir F—— and Father B—— lend to losing Gamesters, that are good Men, and have Fifty in Return.

Ruffles.

By our Fore-fathers call'd Cuffs.

Settee.

The double Pinner. (See Fig. 21.)

47

FIG. 23. A child's dress with hanging bands at the back. A (1695) from the collections at the Nordiska Museum, Stockholm. B from the painting in the National Portrait Gallery of James II's daughter

Sorti.

A little Knot of small Ribbon, peeping out between the Pinner and Bonnet.

Septizonium.

A very high Tower in Rome, built by the Emperour Severus of Seven Ranks of Pillars, set one upon the other, and diminishing to the Top, like the Ladies new Dress for their Heads, which was the mode among the Roman Dames, and is exactly described by Fuvenal in his 6th Satyr.

Tot premit ordinibus, tot adhuc Compagibus altu m Aedificat caput; Andro-machen a fronte videbis Post minor est——

> Such Rows of Curles press'd on each other lye,
> She builds her Head so many Stories high,
> That look on her before, and you would swear
> Hector's tall Wife Andromache she were,
> Behind a Pigmy——

Spanish Paper.

A beautiful red Colour, which the Ladies, &c. in Spain paint their Faces withal.

Spagnolet.

A kind of narrow-sleev'd Gown, a la Spagnole.

Sprunking.

A Dutch term for Pruning, Tiffing, Trimming and setting out, by the Glass or Pocket Miroir.

Sultane.

A gown trimm'd with Buttons, and Loops. (See Figs. 18A and 20A.)

Surtout.

A Night-Hood covering the entire Dress. (See Figs. 18A and 20A.) (Head-dress)

Toilet.

Corruptly call'd the Twilight, but originally signifying a little Cloth.

Tour.

An artificial Dress of Hair on the Forehead, &c.

Tre fine.

Langage de beau. Extremely fine, and delicate, cum multis aliis.

For besides these, there are a world more, as Assasin, or Venez a moy. A certain Breast-knot, as much as to say, Come to me, Sir, &c.

Dutchess. A Knot next the Hair, immediately above the Tour, &c. with innumer-able others now obsolete, and for the present out of use; but we confine ourselves to those in Vogue.

To conclude. Those who have the curiosity, by comparing these Terms with the Ancients, thereby to inform themselves, how this elegant Science is improv'd, especially since we have submitted to, and still continue under the Empire of the French, (for want of some Royal or Illustrious Ladies Invention and Courage, to give the Law of the Mode to her own Country, and to Vindicate it from Foreign Tyranny) may for Divine History consult Isaiah 6th ch. ver. 16, &c. and for Prophane, read Plautus his Poenulus, Act I. Scen. 3 and his Aulularia, Act. 3. Scen. 5.

Chapter III

1700—1720

MEN

IT is extraordinary how quickly the Dutch influence in men's clothes disappeared at the turn of the century and, in spite of the wars with France, the French fashions found their way into this country. The small powdered wig, the full-skirted coat with its high decorated pocket flaps, the laced or fringed long waistcoat, gigantic cuffs, large buttons and buttonholes, stockings gartered and no longer 'rolled'. The black bow tie, full cravat and frilled shirt front, the small lace-edged tricorn hat, antithesis to the gigantic flat hat made necessary by a full bottomed wig.

There is another very good description from Ned Ward's jaundiced pen, of someone pretending to the fashions of the last century:

> . . . 'a demure spark in a diminutive cravat and fox-coloured wig, with a hat as broad as an umbrella, whose level brims revealed that it was carefully preserved in that order by a hatcase and smoothing iron. You might see by his garb that he seems greatly to affect antiquity, though the coat he has on has not been made above this two months; yet he would have it in the ancient mode, with *little buttons, round cuffs, narrow skirts,* and *pockets within two inches of the bottom.*'

The really smart gentleman of this time would be wearing a full-skirted coat, not cut with 'narrow skirts'. He would undoubtedly be wearing scarlet stockings and red-heeled shoes and a lavish cravat made from a whole piece of muslin. He would probably smell strongly of orange-flower water. He would wear a silver-hilted sword and a hat trimmed with silver at the edge of the curled brim, and carry a pair of fringed gloves. His wig would be of the 'night-cap' variety fitting his head snugly and well powdered with starch.

Red and blue were the most fashionable colours—blue coats and scarlet stockings are frequently referred to as smart wear. We can read an inventory of possessions of a lately deceased gentleman in 1709—

> 'A large glass case containing the clothes and linen of the deceased among which are two embroidered suits, a dozen pairs of red-heeled shoes, three pairs of red silk stockings, an amber-headed cane, besides a quart of orange-flower water, a pair of French scissors, a toothpick case, an eyebrow brush and a pocket perspective' (or quizzing glass).

About the same time *The Tatler* comments on the odd dress of country gentlemen, charmingly referring to them as 'Sheep in Wolves Clothing' because of the prevalent fashion in the country to wear scarlet coats for 'best'.

> . . . 'Country gentlemen, who of late years have taken up a humour of coming to town in red coats. . . . Walking in the park I accidentally met a rural esquire, clothed in all the types I mentioned above, with a carriage and behavior made entirely out of his own head. He was of a bulk and stature larger than ordinary, had a red coat, flung open to shew a gay calimanco waistcoat. His periwig fell in a very considerable bush upon each shoulder. His arms naturally swang at an unreasonable distance from his sides; which with the advantage of a cane that he brandished in a great variety of irregular actions, made it unsafe for anyone to walk within several yards of him.'

Red coats at this time usually signified a military uniform, and although they could be worn as described by almost anyone, the immediate reaction to a scarlet coat was that the wearer was an officer in Her Majesty's army.

The cut of the coat, though varied in the first ten years of the eighteenth century, was becoming standardised and the diagrammatic drawings in Chapter IV show just how the full-skirted effect was acquired. The pockets had risen from a few inches above the hem right up to the hip and, in order to defeat pick-pockets, they were all made with loops and buttons. This precaution, however, was by no means foolproof. For we find that the existing coats of that time have rarely had the buttons done up and by about 1730 they were obviously not even made to do up--they had become a mere ornament. The

FIG. 24

waistcoat was made sometimes with sleeves and sometimes without. The sleeved variety (see Figs. 24 and 25) was often worn indoors as a form of 'undress'. Economy was always exercised in the making of the sleeveless type to the extent that only the fronts were decorated, the back was nearly always made from canvas, however rich the material used for the front. Such economy was practised by everybody throughout the century and one can still find the most beautiful brocade gowns and waistcoats with every scrap of material saved that is not going to be seen, and some inferior lining used in its place.

The variety of wigs that were introduced in the early years of the eighteenth century were quite amazing. The first simple tie wig or bag wig was undoubtedly a great deal tidier than the bob wig or the full bottomed, but these comparatively simple arrangements were not worn by the fashionable for long. John Gay gives us further information on wigs and fashion:

... 'sometimes arises a genius in dress who cannot content himself with merely copying from others but will, as he sees occasion, strike out into the long pocket, slashed sleeve, or something particular in the disposition of his lace or the flourish of his embroidery.

... 'On the contrary there are some pretenders to dress who shine out but by halves. A dancing-master of the lowest rank seldom fails of the scarlet stocking and the red heel; and shews a particular respect to the leg and foot to which he owes his subsistence; when at the same time perhaps all the superior ornament of his body is neglected.

... 'Others who lay the stress of beauty in their face, exert all their extravagance in the periwig, which is a kind of index of the mind; the full-bottom formally combed all before, denotes the lawyer and the politician; the smart tye-wig with the black ribbon shows a man of fierceness of temper; and he that burdens himself with a superfluity of white hair which flows down the back, and mantles in waving curls over the shoulders, is generally observed to be less curious in the furniture of the inward recesses of the scull.'

When one realises that the hair had to be cut quite close when wearing these wigs, it is quite obvious that the use of night caps or turbans, when not actually in full dress, was a real necessity. Some of these so-called night caps were made of fur, some borrowed the eastern mode of wearing a turban (see Fig. 24) and there were a great variety of quilted linen, cut leather, velvet and embroidered silks and other decorated night caps all made with a little tuft on top (see

FIG. 25

Fig. 26); usually composed of four segments and a turned-up brim. There is quite a variety in their shapes; probably some men liked them to fit closer round the backs of their necks to give warmth and comfort to the shorn heads, while others preferred something a little more flippant which could be worn with a jaunty air.

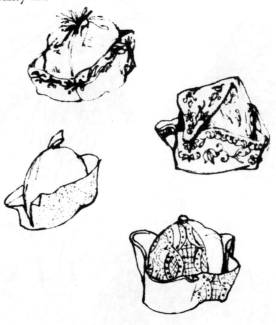

FIG. 26

A complaint to the *Guardian* from a country gentleman just married about the fashions of the day in 1713 runs as follows:

... 'I put myself, according to custom, in another suit, fire-new, with silver buttons to it. I am so out of countenance among my neighbours upon being so fine, that I heartily wish my clothes well worn out. I fancy everybody observes me as I walk the street, and long to be in my old plain geer again. Besides forsooth, they have put me in a silk night-gown and a gaudy fool's cap, and made me now and then stand in the window with it. I am ashamed to be dandled thus, and cannot look in the glass without blushing to see myself turned into such a pretty little master.'

This nightgown means the indoor long coat or dressing gown which was worn over the shirt and breeches to save both the waistcoat from unnecessary wear and tear and the full-skirted coats, which must have been somewhat ungainly as well as rather fragile. These coats incidentally were, a few years after this entry, made with whalebone or wire supports stitched into the side pleats so that they shot out from the waist to their full width in competition with the ladies' vast hooped petticoats.

The differences between full dress and 'plain geer' were remarkable not only in style and cut but in the quality and texture of the materials used. It is unusual to find contemporary records of the plainer and more serviceable garments and fashions. John Gay's Trivia published in 1716 is invaluable from this point of view.

> 'Nor should it prove thy less important Care,
> To chuse a proper Coat for Winter's Wear.
> Now in thy Trunk thy Doily Habit fold,
> The silken Drugget ill can fence the Cold;
> The Frieze's spongy Nap is soak'd with Rain,
> And Show'rs soon drench the Camlet's cockled Grain.
> True Witney Broad-cloath with it's Shag unshorn,
> Unpierc'd is in the lasting Tempest worn:
> Be this the Horse-man's Fence; for who would wear
> Amid the Town the Spoils of Russia's Bear?
> Within the Roquelaure's Clasp thy Hands are pent,
> Hands, that stretch'd forth invading Harms prevent.
> Let the loop'd Bavaroy the Fop embrace,
> Or his deep Cloak be spatter'd o'er with Lace.
> That Garment best the Winter's Rage defends,
> Whose shapeless form in ample Plaits depends;
> By various Names in various Counties known,
> Yet held in all the true Surtout alone:
> Be thine of Kersey firm, though small the Cost,
> Then brave unwet the Rain, unchill'd the Frost.'

Normally the reign of Queen Anne has been considered one of the most outstanding in the history of furniture, architecture and decoration. But somehow the remarkable changes that actually took place in costume at this time have always been attributed to the beginning of the Georgian era. Existing prints of Queen Anne's court quite definitely show the courtly fashions as being somewhat similar to those of the time of William III. But there is no doubt that it was during the middle years of her reign that we find mentioned characteristics which are usually described as Georgian.

The chief of these was the gigantic hoop, or giant petticoat as it was referred to first in 1709 (illustrated in tail piece). Its introduction led to an amusing paper written in *The Tatler* on January 5th, 1710, and ascribed to Addison, wherein a trial was staged and a petticoat brought into court. This petticoat was supposedly lifted over the heads of the audience so that it could be the better criticised. Although one realises that all these papers were exaggerated to make them more amusing, Addison quotes that the hooped petticoat was twenty-four yards in circumference. He also mentions that the common petticoat before the introduction of the hoop was not above four yards in circumference. Various pretended petitions were presented at this same court; one from the rope-makers saying how much they benefited by the use of the cords which were interwoven into the stiffening of the petticoat, another was from the Greenland trade which likewise represented the great consumption of whalebone. A moral plea gently touched upon the weight and unwieldiness of the garment which, it was insinuated, might be of great use to preserve the honour of families. The judge ordered that the petticoat should be folded up and sent as a present to a widow gentle-woman who had five daughters, desiring that she should make each of them a petticoat from it and send back the remainder so that the judge might cut stomachers, caps, facings for his waistcoat sleeves and other garnitures suitable for his age and quality. To conclude the paper the writer says he considers woman as a beautiful romantic animal, that may be adorned with furs and feathers, pearls and diamonds, ores and silks. The lynx shall cast its skin at her feet to make her a tippet; the peacock, parrot and swan shall pay contributions to her muff; the sea shall be searched for shells, and the rocks for gems; and every part of nature furnish out its share towards the embellishment of a creature that is its most consummate work. All this he would indulge them in; but as for the petticoat, he neither could not would allow it.

Apparently breeches, or drawers, were worn under these great hoops, for a short contemporary rhyme on Hoops and High Heels appears in print in 1710.

On Hoops and High Heels

The petticoat's of modest use,
But should a lady chance to fall
The hoop forbidden secrets show.
And Lo' Our eyes discover all.
Then breeches with high heels, I trow,
All hooped modest ladies wear,
For it is plain, these Modes we owe
To Cupid and the culling fair.

The Spectator in 1711, talking of the ladies head-dresses, says:

'. . . within my own memory I have known it rise and fall about thirty degrees. About ten years ago it shot up to a very great height, insomuch as the female part of our species were much taller than the men. (This of course refers to the pinner or commode of the 1690's.) At present the whole sex is in a manner dwarfed and shrunk into a race of beauties that seems almost another species. I remember several ladies who were once very near seven foot high, that at present want some inches of five . . . Those female architects who raise such wonderful structures out of ribbons, lace and wire have not been recorded for their respective inventions.'

Once more we have a definite date for the shrinking of the head-dress, and here again it would seem earlier than is expected. Obviously the flat hair-dressing styles were well established by 1711. Although in many cases the effect was obtained by the tilting forward of the pinner and the removal of a bunch of ribbons or a lace frill—the vague shape of the original bonnet remains until as late as 1726—(a date when a delightful little book of sketches was published giving the head-dresses and wigs seen at court during this year) (see Fig. 27). Elderly ladies and, of course, the less fashionable sort continued to wear the same shaped bonnet as long as they themselves or the bonnet lasted.

FIG. 27.   Bonnets worn at Court, 1726

In *The Tatler* of 1710 there is a supposed advertisement which gives an inventory of clothes stolen during that year; and although quite probably this advertisement is exaggerated, there is no doubt at all that all the listed particulars must have been in everyday use at that time.

'. . . a thick wadded callico wrapper, a musk-coloured velvet mantle lined with squirrel skins, eight night-shifts, four pair of silk stockings curiously darned, six pair of laced shoes, new and old, with the heels of half two inches higher than

FIG. 28. Examples of typical embroideries of 1700–1720. The top design is that on an apron, those at the bottom are a pocket and a stomacher or pectoral. The drawings are taken from the collection at The Gallery of English Costume at Manchester.

their fellows; a quilted petticoat of the largest size, and one of canvas with whale-bone hoops; three pair of stays, bolstered below the left shoulder, two pairs of hips of the newest fashion, six roundabout aprons with pockets (see Fig. 28), and four striped muslin night-rails very little frayed. . . . two leather fore-head-cloths, three pair of oiled dog-skin gloves, seven cakes of superfine Spanish wool, half-a-dozen of Portugal dishes, and a quire of paper from thence; two pair of bran-new plumpers, four black-lead combs, three pair of fashionable

FIG. 29.   Shoes and pattens or overshoes laced and embroidered, typical examples of the ladies' shoes worn during the eighteenth century. The pointed turned-up toe was worn during the first half of the century. The example in the top right corner is a man's shoe.

eyebrows, two sets of ivory teeth, little the worse for wearing, and one pair of box for common use; Adam and Eve in bugle-work, without fig leaves, upon canvas, curiously wrought with her ladyship's own hand; several filligrane curiosities; a crotchet of one hundred and twenty-two diamonds, set strong and deep in silver, with a rump-jewel after the same fashion; bracelet of braided hair, pomander and seed-pearl; a large old purple velvet purse embroidered, and shutting with a spring, containing two pictures in minature, the features invisible.'

Taking each item singly, the whole wardrobe of the lady of fashion appears.

The calico wrapper would be 'undress'—a morning gown to wear about the house; 'A musk-coloured velvet mantle lined with squirrel skins'—a long coat for outdoor wear. Six pair of laced shoes—covered with lace, probably similar to the centre drawing (see Fig. 29). A quilted petticoat of the largest size, and one of *canvas* with *whalebone* hoops—the necessary stiffening for the gigantic skirts which had just come into vogue.

'Two pairs of hips of the newest fashion.' We can safely assume that these were not the gigantic affairs of a later date, but rather the pads worn at the sides that helped to increase the size of a quilted petticoat, often called 'cushions'.

The marvellous collection of toilet articles and beauty aids is intensely amusing—especially the various sets of teeth 'little the worse for wearing'. The 'rump jewel' referred to the ornament that held the skirts up behind before hoops were worn. 'Bran-new plumpers' were the rather revolting little pads worn inside the cheeks to disguise the natural shrinkage from teeth that had been removed.

The deformity mentioned is not unusual at this time—there are many pairs of stays still in existence with pads or bolsters on one side.

As far as I can, I have illustrated all the relevant objects or their nearest counterpart.

About 1710 there was a drastic change in the shape of the stays. It was probably due to the hoops lifting the skirt directly away from the waist that the new style was introduced; for instead of coming down well over the stomach in a V point and elongating the waistline, the point finished a couple of inches below the waist and the shoulder straps became a mere string (see Fig. 30). Such stays were cut almost straight in front and moulded to support the

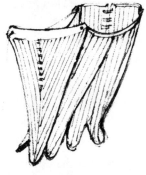

FIG. 30

breasts but force them upward; also the back was lowered. Their solidity was such that any movement was rather startlingly revealing. It was not really the fact of them being so low as the fact of them being so stiff that gave the wearer very little breathing space. If you look at the accompanying drawings it is quite obvious that they were utterly relentless when once laced.

Between 1710 and 1714 the chief criticism seems to have been the fact that the tucker, or frill round the shift, was removed. The contemporary newspapers such as *The Spectator, The Tatler* and *Guardian* give one a very good idea of this fashion. A lengthy correspondence appears in the *Guardian* 1712-13 and Steele does his best to point out the indecencies of the new neckline. The tucker, which was a strip of fine linen or muslin used as a sort of ruffle round the uppermost verge of a woman's stays, had for many years covered a great part of the shoulders and bosom. Steele remarks,

> 'I must take notice that our ladies have of late thrown aside this fig leaf and exposed in its primitive nakedness that gentle swelling of the breasts which it was used to conceal . . . Letting my sight fall upon her bosom, I was surprised with beauties which I never before discovered. The lady observed by my looks that she had made her neck too beautiful an object even for a man of my character and gravity. I could scarce forbear making use of my hand to cover so unseemly a sight.'

Contemporary boastful poems, supposed to have been recorded in St. James' Coffee House, all dwell on this theme.

> 'Last night, as I stood ogling of Her Grace,
> Drinking delicious poison from her face,
> The soft enchantress did her face decline
> Nor ever raised her eyes to meet with mine;
> With sudden art some secret did portend
> Leaned 'cross two chairs to whisper to a friend,
> While the stiff whalebone with the motion, rose
> A thousand beauties to my sight exposed.'

'Cosins' was the popular stay maker of this time and an amusing short poem written in 1715 reads as follows:

> 'She owes to me the very charms she wears:
> An awkward thing when first she came to town;
> Her shape unfashioned and her face unknown.
> She was my friend, I taught her first to spread,
> Upon her sallow cheeks enlivening red.

I introduced her to the Park and plays:
And by my interest Cosins made her stays.
Ungrateful wretch! with mimic air grown pert,
She dares to steal my favourite lover's heart.'

Another story refers to the stays of this same period. They were, as I have already described, very hard and difficult to get into quickly, and their main purpose was to keep the bodice of the gown firm and trim so that no unseemly bulge should interfere with the fashionable symmetry. In order to achieve this effect, there were lacings both front and back, although the front ones were never unlaced, and after a time, were practically sealed.

When Lady Mary Wortley Montague—one of our best sources for foreign fashion of the time—was in Turkey in 1717, she visited the Turkish baths of a harem to see the ladies disporting themselves; she was enchanted with their attractions, and apparently they were slightly disconcerted that she didn't join them in their ablutions. Eventually several of them endeavoured by signs to suggest she disrobed . . .

'I was, at last, forced to open my skirt and show them my stays; which satisfied them very well, for I saw they believed I was so locked up in that machine that it was not in my power to open it, which contrivance they attributed to my husband.'

Writing from Vienna in 1716 she mentions the great size of the petticoats '. . . their whalebone petticoats outdo ours by several yards circumference and cover some acres of ground'. They were also still outlandishly large in the 'fifties when Maria Teresa was queen.

In 1718 Paris fashions were still surprising and provocative:

'. . . I must tell you something of French ladies, so fantastically absurd is their dress, so monstrously unnatural is their paint. Their hair is cut short and curled round their faces, loaded with powder which makes it look like white wool, and on their cheeks to their chin unmercifully laid on a shining red japan that glisters in a most flaming manner. They seem to have no resemblance to human faces . . . thus with pleasure I recollect my dear, pretty countrywomen and if I was writing to any body else I should say that these grotesque daubers give me a still higher esteem of the natural charms of dear Lady R——'s auburn hair and the lively colours of her unsullied complexion.'

Apparently at this date English ladies did not powder their hair. It was sufficient that they wore their little caps of fine point lace or minunet or even blonde.

The same correspondent writes the following amusing anecdote, which gives us an insight of the expense incurred and the trouble taken to obtain a really good French 'head' or bonnet.

When travelling back from Paris, she encountered an Englishwoman on the boat who was endeavouring to smuggle lace.

> . . . 'She had bought a fine point-head, which she was contriving to conceal from the customs house officers. When the wind grew high, and our little vessel rocked, she fell heartily to her prayers. . . . "Dear Madam, will you take care of this point?—if it should be lost—Ah, Lord, we shall all be lost!—Lord have mercy on my soul! Pray, Madam, take care of this head-dress." '

Obviously the value of point lace ranked almost as high as life itself. Such little bits of lace head-dress and lace generally were extremely expensive, partly because of the duty on such imports but also because of the immense amount of time hand-made lace takes to make.

Lady Stafford in 1721 asked for 'one suit of minunet for head and ruffles at Boileau's'. This suit of minunet or mignonnette was a small lace priced at a guinea a yard but probably twice that price in England.

During the period when Lady Mary or her sister were in France, there was a continual stream of requests from friends and relations to send or bring back purchases from the Paris shops. Such purchases not only included lace of sorts but such everyday items as —'A made-up mantua', a 'petticoat of Rat de St. Maur', 'A night gown ready-made', 'twenty yards of black lutestring', 'French trimming—a slight pretty thing for a guinea', etc.

There are several etceteras which appear as the insignia of a certain kind of behaviour. One of these is the mask. At certain periods in the history of costume the mask was an everyday covering for the face, worn rather as a protection from sun or wind, than for any more coquettish reason. It was during Queen Anne's reign that the mask became a badge of prostitution because 'it conferred a certain degree of invisibility and concealed many immoralities'. Indeed, masks simply tended to degenerate into an opportunity for people to behave as they felt inclined without disclosing their identity.

The umbrella, contrary to general belief, was used in the streets of England at the beginning of the century. Again quoting from Gay's *Trivia or the Art of Walking the Streets of London*, printed in 1716 and probably written earlier:

> 'Good Huswives all the Winter's Rage despise,
> Defended by the Riding-hood's Disguise;
> Or underneath th' Umbrella's oily Shed,
> Safe thro' the Wet on clinking Pattens tread.
> Let Persian Dames th' Umbrella's Ribs display,
> To guard their Beauties from the sunny Ray:
> Or sweating Slaves support the shady Load,
> When Eastern Monarchs shew their State abroad;
> Britain in Winter only knows its Aid,
> To guard from chilly Show'rs the walking Maid.'

Even earlier than that we find quoted in *The Tatler* of 1710, 'The tucked-up seamstress walks with natty stride, while streams run down her oiled umbrella's side.' By this we can safely assume that the umbrella was certainly used by pedestrian women, though in all probability it would be a useless etcetera for a lady of fashion; umbrellas and hooped pettitcoats are an incongruous combination. The fan, again, is an item of importance which must not be omitted from the well-dressed lady's toilet. The fans in Queen Anne's time were not very large, varying from between nine and twelve inches when folded. They could be made from lace, hand-painted parchment or fine embroidery. There was a great deal in the art of using fans. Such art not only included creating a breath of air, it could be used as a weapon of defence or provocation, or even something to look at when at a loss for polite conversation.

There were dozens of other items of interest in a ladies' wardrobe, not the least of them being the hood. These hoods naturally were very large as long as the pinner was high, and gave a curious elongated effect to the face, but as the bonnet became smaller the hoods became more frivolous, and by 1712 the fashion for coloured hoods included every possible shade except black which was only used for mourning. A mention in *The Spectator* was followed by an attempt at analysis—always a problematical conjecture as far as women are concerned! . . .

> 'I am informed that this fashion spreads daily, insomuch that the Whig and Tory ladies begin already to hang out different colours, and to shew their principles in their head-dress. . . . "My friend Will tells me he can already guess at the humour a lady is in by her hood; . . . in flame colour, her heart is set upon execution. When she covers it with purple, I would not, says he, advise her lover to approach her; but if she appears in white, it is peace, and he may hand her out of her box with safety.
>
> 'Will informs me likewise that these hoods may be used as signals. Why else does Cornelia always put on a black hood when her husband is gone into the country?'

A year before Queen Anne's death the hoop petticoat changed its shape. A contemporary reference reads

> '. . . they still resolutely persist in this fashion. The form of their bottom is not, I confess, altogether the same; for whereas before it was of an orbicular make, they now look as if they were pressed, so that they seem to deny access to any part but the middle. Many are the inconveniences that accrue to her Majesty's loving subjects by the said petticoats, as hurting men's shins, sweeping down the wares of industrious females in the streets, etc. I saw a young lady fall down the other day; and believe me Sir, she very much resembled an over-turned bell, without a clapper. Many are the disasters I could tell you of that befall themselves as well as others by means of this unwieldy garment.'

About the same time we find a reference to shorter skirts, 'which grow shorter and shorter every day. The leg discovers itself in proportion to the neck.'

In Figure 31 we have a picture of a fashionable lady in Queen Anne's time with the characteristic silhouette associated with Hogarth's drawings—some thirty years later. (See Fig. 31.)

Except in a variety of small details the fashions remained very much the same during those thirty years; there are of course several exaggerations and innovations which do not actually interfere with the now established Georgian

FIG. 31

silhouette, but on the whole, from about 1714 to 1740, both men's and women's dress retained the characteristics already mentioned.

The remarkable features of the next thirty years were either foreign extravagances, or else the growing interest in design, both embroidery design and the gradually changing styles of fabric weaving—the full-skirted petticoats, coats and waistcoats were an excellent groundwork for such display—and in the following pages vivid contemporary descriptions, each outvying the other, will be found.

We have seen how with the turn of the century a revolution in silhouette had set in, and within a short ten years the whole population of civilised Europe had altered its formal elongated look to one of rotundity. Great petticoats and tiny heads took the place of high heads and trailing skirts. The skirts to men's coats vied in pleated magnificence with the voluminous petticoats of the women. Full-bottomed wigs became an old-fashioned joke and the close-fitting night-cap wig competed for smallness with the neat perched-up hair styles that Watteau found so enchanting in the ladies.

This revolution was enthusiastically watched and recorded by dozens of contemporary writers, and before the close of Queen Anne's reign the 'new look' had come to stay, and stay it did, with various modifications, for more than a quarter of a century.

Quite naturally with such an exaggerated structure for full dress, 'undress' developed into a fine art. A carefully studied nonchalance could display to the full the elegance of a laced shirt—a casually tied cravat might show more lace than a formal arrangement. An Indian nightgown, or a sleeved waistcoat for informal wear could be both elegant and comfortable and the embroidered night-cap might be as frivolous or sedate and cosy as required.

Women's 'undress' provided them with an excuse to discard both stays and hoops—always remembering that the shift was a very voluminous garment. The sleeves full and frilled, the snugly fitting wadded waistcoat showed off the frilly edge at neck and the wide laced sleeves to their best advantage. The quilted petticoats, enchantingly patterned in themselves, sprang from the waistcoat flaps like the petals of a fritillary falling from the perianth (see Figs. 32 and 17). The 'contouche', a large all enveloping gown, could be both warm and accommodating to an unlaced lady.

70

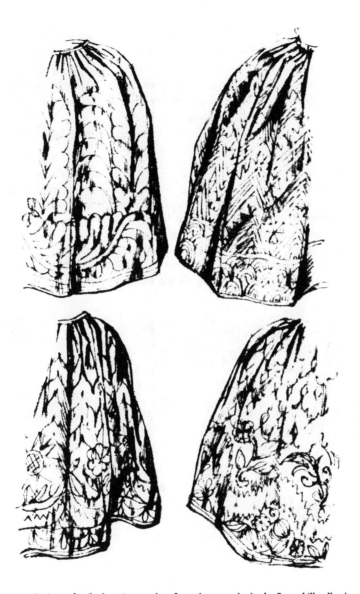

FIG. 32. Designs of quilted petticoats taken from the examples in the Snowshill collection

There was every excuse to adopt the fashion for entertaining one's friends while dressing so that the full range of 'undress' could be appreciated by an audience. In the higher status of society the toilet occupied several hours; business was often transacted and appointments and social engagements made, whilst a barber or ladies' maid was in attendance.

Writings of the period include the following description of this social function:

'It is a very odd sight that beautiful creature makes, when she is talking politics with her tresses flowing about her shoulders, and examining that face in the glass, which does such execution upon all the male standers-by. How prettily does she divide her discourse between her woman and her visitants? What sprightly transitions does she make from an opera or a sermon to an ivory comb or a pin-cushion? How have I been pleased to see her interrupted in an account of her travels, by a message to her footman; and holding her tongue in the midst of a moral reflection, by applying the tip of it to a patch?'

Chapter IV

1720—1750

THERE is no better illustrator of these particular thirty years than Hogarth, and the picture of male fashions remains very much the same: the long waistcoat still half way down the thigh—just a trifle shorter as the middle of the century approaches—the full-skirted coat, wired or stiffened at the pleats during the 'thirties and 'forties in an effort to compete with the vast hoops of the fashionable ladies (see illustration at top of page).

Coats, waistcoats and breeches were often made to match, but the 'laced' waistcoat was usually a thing apart. A magnificent specimen of silver lace, still untarnished and mounted on a brilliant saffron-yellow watered tabby is the example here illustrated. The lace is heavy and could easily be removed from one garment to another. (Fig. 33.)

When riding, the skirts of the coats were usually pinned or buttoned back to the centre buttons just below the waist; this fashion started during the 'thirties and as a part of the military uniform outlasted the century.

French fashions and a French accent were considered very elegant, and the way in which a cuff or ruffle was flicked, a cane used, or a snuff box or quizzing glass handled, was often of more telling quality than the garments themselves.

'Well may we laugh at laws which you intrench
Whose equipage and politicks are French;
Your dress, your airs, and all your modes of fashion
Borrow'd from that fantastick idle nation!'

FIG. 33

It was really the wigs that gave variety to this era, and there were dozens of amusing styles which occur, from the absurd little white wig with a 'fluke' or pigtail to the gigantic full-bottomed wig still cherished by the elderly country gentleman or the 'Bob-wig' which was even worn as late as the 'seventies and 'eighties.

FIG. 34

The peculiarities of fashions in wigs were well illustrated in a charming little sketch-book by Bernard Lens (now in the Print Room of the Victoria and Albert Museum). These drawings were done at court and show the very latest styles in wig-making that appeared in 1725-1726. Nor do they only show the actual wig, for they illustrate a variety in cravats and neck ribbons both unexpected and amusing (Fig. 34).

75

The peruke maker was not having such a good time as one might expect with such an endless source of income at his fingertips. The authorities were becoming apprehensive of various shortages of materials that were daily being absorbed for the dressing of wigs, and in June 1731 the following act was introduced.

'That foresoafter June 24th 1731 if any maker of hair powder, perfumes, peruke maker or barber shall mix any powder of alabaster, plaster of Paris, talc, chalk, whiting, lime or any other materials (rice first made into starch and sweet scents only excepted) with starch or powder of starch to be mixed for hair powder; or shall use, sell or offer to sell powder so mixed, shall forfeit the said powder and the sum of twenty pounds. That all dealers in hair powder, having in their possession any of the materials hereby prohibited shall forfeit the said materials and ten pounds.'

This was followed by a precautionary notice that at the next chief Office of Excise all places of abode and wash houses were likely to be visited and a penalty of £20 fine imposed if anyone was found contravening the law.

Wigs generally were more varied than any other item of clothing, there were fashions and freaks to suit the most difficult client. Although the elderly still clung to the fashion of their youth and certain professions adopted certain types of wigs, the more frivolous younger generation blossomed out in the oddest shapes. They seemed to grow curious tufts and horns and were probably at their most ridiculous during the 'thirties and 'forties, when the long fluke or pig-tail shot out from the back of the head in a half circle, and tortoiseshell combs were stuck into the hair in the front, giving rather the impression of a barber's wig imperfectly finished. In the *Gentleman's Magazine* of 1731 the following extract gives a very good idea at the messiness of a would-be fashionable man without knowledge or elegance.

'Stalking along with the harness of the dullest Englishman, his dress imitating the pert gaiety of a Frenchman. View him no higher than the shoulder, you would take him for a meal man who has just done his work and has not had the time to brush the flour from off his coat. The hind part of the head resembles a Mercury, with a pair of wings fastened to his cap. One waggish lady would not allow them the name of wings but called them asses ears.'

In the same magazine appears the following description of elegant young manhood.

'Fops—a parcel of spruce, powdered fopling, with their hair tucked under a tortoiseshell comb, their sleeves flicked up above their elbows, a gold-headed cane in one hand and an agate box in 'tother, with a nose full of snuff and a head full of—nothing.'

One of the most interesting references to men's wigs occurs when, in the year 1751, Lady Mary Wortley Montague's son is reputed to have brought back from Paris an iron wig, apparently something in fine iron wire. This is mentioned in Elizabeth Montague's letters, 'He brought from Paris an iron wig; you literally would not know it from real hair.'

About 1740 the knee-breeches which had usually been worn inside the stocking were reversed, and the stocking worn inside with the breeches buttoning over. This is, however, a variable date, for there are many drawings earlier than 1740 when the common man is shown with his breeches outside the stocking (Fig. 35).

There are many references to the odd effect that one might see in the streets any day of the week. Such things as discoloured wigs, powdered shoulders, the wearing

Fig. 35

of 'night gowns' or waistcoats rather than coats, nightcaps and turbans too, in fact, all the 'undress' attire that might more reasonably be expected indoors found its way into common use.

Elizabeth Montague writing in 1745 describes the following:

'He had on a grey striped calamanco nightgown, a wig that once was white but by the influence of uncertain climate turned to a pale orange, a brown hat, black hatband; a band somewhat dirty that decently retired under his chin; a pair of grey stockings, well mended with blue worsted.'

Flowered fustians were much in vogue for those who could not afford the more magnificent extravagances in cloth or silk, and in 1731, at a famous hanging, the hangman rode to the execution in a suit of flowered fustian, presented him by the master weavers in contempt of foreign manufacturers.

There was a great deal of high feeling at this time about imported fabrics, their impracticability and their fragile quality being frequently referred to. Taken from the *Gentleman's Magazine* of 1743 is the following 'Economical Reflection'.

'All mortal things are frail—and go to pot.
What wonder then, if mortal trowsers rot?
My Velvet torn, I shone in mimick Shagg;
Those soon grew rusty and—began to flag.
Buck-skin was greasy; Serge de Nym was queer;
Camblet was airy; but how apt to tear!
Quoth, I; Sir Pricklouse, shall we try a Rug?
Yes, Sir, says he! that sure,—will hold a tug.
Ah! no; the Rug decay'd, like all the past,
Even Everlasting would not everlast.
At length; guess how I fix'd it.—why, in troth,
With projects tir'd—I stuck to common cloth.'

In 1748, the Prince of Wales appeared in a procession wearing a sky-blue watered tabby coat, with gold buttonholes and a magnificent gold waistcoat, fringed, leading Madame l'Ambassadine de Venise in a green sac with a straw hat.

Descriptions of court balls and birthdays give us other ideas of colour, and curiously enough the colours worn in candle-light all seem to be much softer than those worn for daylight functions.

The following descriptions all tend towards shades of brown. In 1738,

FIG. 36. Diagram for cutting the full skirted coat. The cross on the shoulder indicates the weave of the material

'There was nothing extraordinary among the men but much finery, chiefly brown with gold and silver embroidery and rich waistcoats.' Again in 1739, 'My Lord Baltimore was in light brown and silver, his coat lined quite throughout with ermine.'

This apparent quietness of colour played a dual purpose. For not only was it the perfect neutral background for the brilliant embroideries that were coming into vogue, but it acted as a foil for the true magnificence of the ladies' vast hooped skirts covered with brilliant designs.

The use of fur as a lining is also an interesting feature of this era and apparently it was worn by both sexes. A letter of 1742 gives a brilliant picture of a full court.

'I have dined two days together in Arlington Street, but heard no discourse than what tended to the finery of yesterday. My Lord C. was in plain cloth: ('tis well if his heart had the simplicity of his garment,) which was what it appeared to be a good warm, clean, coat. My lady was in dark green velvet trimmed with ermine, and an ermine petticoat—a present from her son, but it would have better suited the slender-waisted daughter Fanny, who had a scarlet damask and all her mother's jewels, was very well dressed, and became her clothes. I have not seen her look so well. Mrs. Spencer was in blue and silver. But our fair Maid of Honour outshone them all; clad in rich pink satin trimmed with silver, more blooming and dazzling than anything there except her own complexion; she was perfectly well dressed, and looked so modest and unaffected, that I think I never saw a more agreeable figure; in the evening I went to Lady North's, where I saw but few people. The Duchess of Montrose was in silver tissue; Lady Scarborough in blue damask with a gold trimming. There were several very handsome flowered silks, shaded like embroidery; but the finest clothes were Lady Caroline Lenox's, gold and colours on white, embroidered by Mrs Wright.'

Drawings of ladies' head-dress in 1726 appear in the sketch book, already referred to, by Bernard Lens, and show the interesting development of the bonnet at the beginning of the century into the little cap or 'mob' of a later date (see Fig 27). What obviously happened was that many ladies found it convenient to wear the same bonnets with the pinner frill much smaller and the bonnet pushed forward on to the top of the head rather than at the back as it had been at an earlier date. It is curious that this stiffened frill should have lasted for so many years and that the 'streamers' should have also existed, for surely the streamers on a maid's bonnet in the nineteenth century had the same origin.

One amusing idea seems to have been that of folding up the streamers on top of the bonnet to form a little pleated pile on top of the head (see Fig. 27, top right). Watteau shows this curious fashion in one or two of his charming back views of young ladies.

During the 'thirties there were once again some heated and scathing comments on the low neckline, dictated by the French fashions. A contemporary record of the latest fashions was as follows: 1734 . . . 'They (the French) wear their stays extravagantly low, their sleeves very short and wide, petticoats short, English "dormeuses" and the girdle (waistline) not in the least peaked down. . . .'

However, the English fashions counteracted this difficulty by wearing a kerchief or scarf pinned to the bodice with buckles and a strap or ribbon between. There are frequent references to these buckles as 'Buckles for her stays', and they formed quite a definite item in dress for some fifteen years, and even longer with the more old-fashioned and sedate (see Fig. 38). In 1736 the *Gentleman's Magazine* remarked on this fashion:

FIG. 37. Capucin and hat, 1726

'and when the mode deprives women of part of their covering before and exposes half their breast to public view it becomes a modest lady, though she conforms as near as she can to the fashion in stays, to correct the immodesty of the mode with a neck cloth or handkerchief and hide certain bewitching allurements from a curious eye. Notwithstanding that she may have reason to suspect her modesty will be misinterpreted to the disadvantage of her neck.'

FIG. 38. A variety of hoops and panniers worn between 1720–1750. All these are to be found in various collections in England

The tapering quality of the stays during the 'twenties and 'thirties obviously had done much to provoke this display of breast. The shape changed for the worse during the 'forties. Contemporary references show us that the stays did not enhance the feminine waist. In 'forty-one, when the hoops were very large, a mother writing to her daughter said,

> 'I do not know what will become of your shape for there is a fashion-make (of stays) that is very strange. I believe they look in London as they did in Rome after the rape of the Sabines.'

These stays were made with a very heavy busk in the front, triangular in section and sometimes half an inch or more deep, which naturally made the waist appear wider than necessary but gave more support to the top of the stays. That they were difficult to get into and out of was remarked in an amusing confession of Horace Walpole's in 1742, when he went to a masque as an old woman. . . 'I was so awkward at undressing myself that I had stood for an hour in my stays and under petticoat before my footman.'

In 1738 hoops were supplied at 14 guineas a time, made to the exact dimensions of an old one. According to Hogarth's pictures, the petticoat reached its greatest proportions in about 'forty-one. (Figs. 38 and 39.)

A letter written to London in 'forty-one reads as follows:

> 'I should be obliged to you if you would in your next letter send me word what size hoops moderate people, who are neither over lavish nor covetous of whalebone, wear. Because I intend to write to my hoop-maker and have one ready for me against I come to Town. I don't care to leave the size of it to her discretion. I hope our hoops will not increase much more for we are already about as unreasonable as Queen Dido and don't encircle much less with our whalebone than she did with her bull's hide.'

(This is presumably a reference to Dido's marking out the boundary of the city of Carthage with strips of bull's hide.) In 'forty-two, again quoting from the same letters:

> 'Mrs. Rook . . . is just come from France and is come without a hoop, and tells me that except in their high dress nobody wears one. Their sacs are made proportionately narrow and short, opened before with a petticoat and trimmed, and with a stiff quilted petticoat under. This is the only reasonable thing I have

heard from France in a great while and the only fashion I wish to follow.' (See Fig. 42.)

This gives us a definite date for the first collapse of the hooped petticoat in France, and though one finds frequent references to them at a later date, they were in all probability more fashionable as hip hoops, instead of the whole whalebone and canvas petticoat. The Duchess of Queensbury, so frequently referred to as the greatest beauty of her age in this country, is mentioned in 1743 in a charming undress.

> . . . 'Who should glide in but the Duchess of Queensbury in a mob and white hood pinned close under her chin, a yellow mohair gown, no ruffles only little frills sewed to her shift, no hoop, a tumbled apron and her capuchin dangling round her arm; yet there was a grace in her altogether that shone out in spite of her dress.'

Another interesting commentary in the *Gentleman's Magazine* of 1736 criticised the make-up in France and showed that there was still considerable excess in this particular.

> 'In France, the centre and school of the arts of living, the women are about equally beautiful and 'tis difficult to make distinction though at never so little distance. Those who are indebted to nature for fair skin, find themselves obliged to lay on red. Those to whom nature has not been so liberal, make no difficulty in daubing their skin all over and, if white is not sufficient, they add blue and streak their veins with it. So that nothing is left for real beauty to distinguish itself to advantage from what is sophisticate. The art of daubing is not yet fashionable among us, but if our fine ladies be not well upon their guard, I fear they will soon be bubbled out of their natural advantages. . . . What difference is there between the cleanest limbed body and the most clumsy shape when covered with a sack? A fine lady is never more agreeable than in her undress and nothing adds greater charm to her beauty than the long tresses of well-nourished hair loosely flowing about her shoulders and breasts. But those who have not an equal share of this advantage have found out the envious artifice to depose their rivals of this natural charm by obliging them to conceal it. So that art which was designed to be the servant and assistant to nature takes at present the reins of government into her hands and insolently straps nature as a chained captive at the wheels of her triumphant chariot.'

FIG. 39.   Examples of very large side hoops and coat cut to accommodate them, 1725–1730

We can see clearly the reason for such criticism contained in the last paragraph, for the fashions of the 'thirties were not at their most charming. The hair was still packed up tightly under a cap, neither so becoming as the little ones of the 'twenties, nor so decorative as those of the 'forties. The fashion tended to

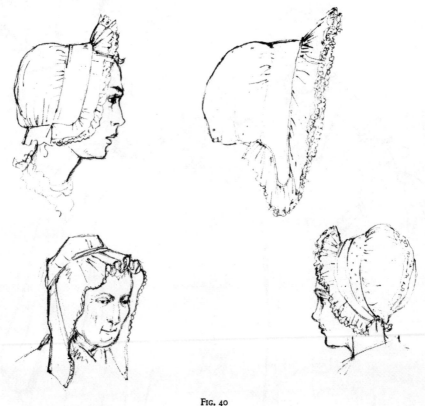

FIG. 40

make all faces rounder than necessary by the rather austere dragging back of the hair. By about 1740 curls were again worn. The sacks also were not at their best for they still hung loosely from the shoulders and were not yet moulded on to a fitted lining at the back.

86

The wearing of 'heads' or bonnets was still general during the 'forties. Few ladies appeared in public without some sort of lacy nonsense pinned in their hair. The 'mob', seemingly so dear to theatrical productions, was not as generally worn as is supposed. Nor was it a circle of material gathered into a frill! It was a word used to describe a bonnet, more often with lappets and edged with lace, than a cambric cap (see Fig. 40).

Talking of correct dress to her daughter, a mother advises,

'I think you quite right to make a sack; they are easier and handsomer than any other dress for a lady in your circumstances; you may wear a sac with a mob under your chin if you please. Scotch caps are all the mode and worn by all ages, they are put on with a couplé of pins and that is a great recommendation for any dress.'

These Scotch caps were not necessarily plaid, though they were roughly of the Glengarry shape, with little ribbons hanging down behind. Point lace, bone lace and blonde (the cheapest form of lace) were used in the daytime almost to the exclusion of anything else. For full-dress occasions the hair was more often dressed with pom-poms or aigrettes, or some decorative arrangement of precious stones and flowers, or imitation flowers, held in place by gold or silver wires. At this time the capuchin was worn almost to the exclusion of the ordinary hood. It must be remembered that elderly ladies still retained the style of head-dresses that they had worn in their youth. Therefore we nearly always see portraits of women in their sixties and seventies with some form of goffered frill, vaguely reminiscent of the pinner, worn over the forehead. Most of these bonnets also still retained the long lappets on either side of the face that can be pinned beneath the chin. Straw hats with small crowns and a brim of almost any width were worn over the bonnet and usually tied on, sometimes with a ribbon that went round the back of the head and sometimes for security's sake under the chin.

Elizabeth Montague writes of a gathering in 1745:

'Such hats, capuchins and short sacs as were never seen. One of the ladies looks like a state bed running upon castors—she had robbed the valence and tester of a bed for trimming.'

The short sacs were probably similar to the one illustrated (Fig. 41).

It is interesting to notice that, as weaving and brocading developed a variety of complicated colourings, the fashion for embroideries became larger and larger in an effort to differentiate between a woven and a hand-embroidered garment. One finds in the records of fashionable gatherings for such things as the Royal Birthdays, the most enlightening descriptions of competitive designs. In 1734 a description of a brocaded lute-string, to be worn at the Royal wedding,

'is a white ground with great rambling flowers in shades of purples, reds and greens. I gave thirteen shillings a yard; it looks better than it describes and will make a show. I shall wear with them dark purple and gold ribbon and a black hood for decency's sake.'

Eighteen yards of material were necessary for a gown at this date and in some instances one repeat covered the full width of the material; such as this described in a letter from Mrs. Pendarves to Ann Granville in 1739:

FIG. 41

'After much persuasion and many debates within myself, I consented to go with Lady Dysart to the Prince's birthday, humbly drest in my pink damask, white and gold handkerchief, plain green ribbon, and Lady Sunderland's buckles for my stays. I was a good foil for those that were there. I never saw so much finery without any mixture of trumpery in my life. Lady Huntingdon's, as the most extraordinary, I must first describe—her petticoat was black velvet embroidered with chenille, the pattern a large stone vase filled with ramping flowers that spread almost over a breadth of the petticoat from the bottom to the top; between each vase of flowers was a pattern of gold shells, and foliage embossed and most heavily rich; the gown was white satin embroidered also with chenille mixt with gold ornaments, no vases on the sleeve, but two or three on the tail; it was a most laboured piece of finery, the pattern much properer for a stucco staircase than the apparel of a lady,—a mere shadow that tottered under every step she took under the load. The next fine lady was Mrs. Spencer; her clothes, green paduasoy covered all over, the gown as well as petticoat, with a very fine and very pretty trimming; it was well made; she looked genteel and easy, and had all the dowager Duchess of M's jewels, which made her look quite magnificent. Lady Dysart was white gold, and looked as handsome as ever I saw her; Miss Carteret in an uncut blue velvet, and all my Lady Carteret's jewels; Lady Carteret in the same clothes she made for the Prince's wedding, white and gold and colours; the Princess was in white satin, the petticoat covered with a gold trimming like embroidery, faced and robed with the same. Her head and stomacher a rock of diamonds and pearls; her looks pleased me better than her dress;'

In the following January was another description from the same pen:

'The Duchess of Bedford's petticoat was green paduasoy, embroidered very richly with gold and silver and a few colours; the pattern was festoons of shells, coral, corn, corn-flowers, and sea-weeds; everything in different works of gold and silver except the flowers and coral, the body of the gown white satin, with a mosaic pattern of gold facings, robings and train the same as the petticoat; there was abundance of embroidery, and many people in gown and petticoats of different colours.'

The reference to the gown and petticoat of different colours is an interesting landmark, for previously it is often difficult to see in a painting or drawing where the skirts of the gown finish and the petticoat begins.

The use of chenille for decoration gave the design an added substance in much the same way as the so-called 'Stump Work' embroideries, so typical of

FIG. 42. Scarlet and white brocade sac and petticoat in the Snowshill collection

the seventeenth century, projected their designs into relief. The frequent mentions of robings and facings refer to the edgings and decorations on the gown and stomacher, often gold or silver lace and in the simpler dresses composed entirely of pleated strips of material cut with pinking shears and twined in a variety of patterns. A delightful economy exists in the simpler garments of taffety, for the pinked facings are so arranged that no hem was required— the weight of the decorations was sufficient to keep the skirts in place, and the pinking was efficient enough to stop the fabric unravelling. Even some of the more expensive gowns have this form of decoration. There is a beautiful example in the Snowshill collection, as shown in Fig. 42.

A profuse contemporary letter-writer, Mrs. Pendarves excels in descriptions, and one more written in 'forty-one is too good to miss:

'I will proceed to give you an account of our doings at Norfolk House. I told you what my clothes were. Dash went with me, she was in pale pink and silver very well drest, and looked like the picture of Modesty; we went at half an hour after one. I never saw so full a Court, the Prince was in black velvet, the Princess in white and gold and colours, a very fine rich stuff. She looked very majestic and well, and acquitted herself, as she always does, with great propriety. My Lady Scarborough was in violet-coloured satin, the petticoat embroidered with clumsy festoons of *nothing at all's supported by pillars* no better than posts, the gown covered with embroidery, a very unmeaning pattern, but altogether very fine. Lady Cobham and the Duchess of Bedford in rich gold stuff. Lady Bruce, in lemon colour richly embroidered with silver and colours, a small pattern; Lady M. Tufton white embroidered with garlands and *flower-pots* of flowers mixt with a great deal of silver, it cannot be described so well as it looked, for it was handsome; Lady Godschall had on a suit of clothes that were designed for her *in case she had been Lady Mayoress*, white satin embroidered with gold and browns, very fine.

The Duchess of Queensbury's clothes pleased me best; they were white satin embroidered, the bottom of the petticoat *brown hills* covered with all sorts of weeds, and *every breadth* had *an old stump of a tree* that run up almost to the top of the petticoat, broken and ragged and worked with brown chenille, round which twined nasturtiums, ivy honeysuckles, periwinkles, convolvuluses and all sorts of twining flowers which spread and covered the petticoat, vines with the leaves variegated as you have seen them by the sun, all rather smaller than nature,

91

which made them look very light; the robings and facings were little green banks
with all sorts of weeds, and the sleeves and the rest of the gown loose twining
branches of the same sort as those on the petticoat; many of the leaves were
finished with gold, and part of the stumps of the trees looked like the gilding of
the sun. I never saw a piece of work so prettily fancied, and am quite angry with
myself for not having the same thought, for it is infinitely handsomer than mine,
and could not cost *much more*; these were the finest ladies. Lady Carteret was in
an ugly flowered silk on a dirty yellow ground, Miss Carteret in pale pink satin
and *very glorious with jewels*; Mrs. Spencer in a white flowered velvet very dull,
but *all* the Duchess of Marlborough's jewels; Lady Dysart did not go, nor Lady
Catherine Hanmer, though she had bought clothes; my Lady Egmont's brother
died three weeks ago, and my lady out of perverseness would not let her go,
for nobody observes forms for an uncle after they are buried. The ball was
begun at nine, by the Prince and Princess, and lasted till I was tired of the number
that sailed about. The finest man was Lord Annandale, who is just come home;
he is very tall, and what is called handsome, and much commended for his
dancing. The men in general were not remarkably fine. Dash, by a mistake of
her mantua-maker's was spoiled for a dancer; but she danced country dances
with Sir Francis Dashwood, who stuck by us all night, and is a very entertaining
man. We left the great crowd at one, and when I came home I found your
letter.'

A letter from Lady Dysart to Mrs. Delany in 1748 described her sister's
trousseau:

'I think my sister Fanny to all appearance happily established; the Marquis
is a sensible reasonable man, and quite her lover. He has £4000 a year in Scotland
and two houses—one of them, I am told, is a very fine place; my sister has £1200
a year jointure rent-charge. He has given her a very fine pair of brilliant earrings,
one drop, a girdle buckle, and five stars for her stays; her clothes (she was
married in) were white satin flounced, with a magnificent silver trimming all
over the gown and petticoat; she had besides a white and gold with colours, a
pink and silver sac, a brocaded lutestring gown and petticoat, a white satin
sultane with embroidered robings of natural flowers, and a pink and white
sprigged sultane. I have now told you all her clothes; her lace was fine and well
chosen, her best head was point. The Marquis has the house in Grosvenor Street
where Sir Robert Hide lived: they don't go to Scotland this year.'

Chapter V

1750—1775

ONLY two descriptions of men's Court clothes occur in Mrs. Delany's enchanting letters between the years 1750 and 1775. The letter of 1753 gives us a date for the early satin embroidered waistcoats that were to be so very fashionable for the next twenty or thirty years. The coat, again in tones of grey-brown, could be the description of a dozen or more Court coats still in museum collections.

> 'The Duke went, and was very fine; his coat dark mouse-coloured velvet, embroidered with silver; Jenny Glegg's work, and the finest I ever saw; the waistcoat Isabella satin, embroidered the same as the coat; there was a great deal of finery . . .'

In 1773, twenty years later, we see a picture of one of the more exotic type. There were many of these very expensive coats, ornamented with mirrors, jewels and sequins, and it was during the 'seventies and 'eighties that ornament added to embroidery became so fashionable.

> 'The chief topick of conversation yesterday was Lord Villiers' appearance in the morning at Court in a pale purple velvet coat, turned up with lemon-colour, and embroidered all over with S.S.'s of pearl as big as pease, and in all the spaces little medallions in beaten gold, *real solid*, in various figures of Cupids and the like.'

During the 'seventies it was unusual to wear a waistcoat of the same material as the coat, and cream or pastel-coloured satin embroidered in a variety of colours was suitable with almost any coloured suit.

Ordinary coats and breeches were made from plain materials, such as felt and jersey and various types of woollen weave, for summer wear taffety, fustian, tabby, etc., with perhaps embroidery on the buttons.

For many years the coat had been getting shorter, tighter and more and

more cut away, and at the close of this particular period (1770–1775) the fronts were cut away so much that the waistcoat must show on all occasions (see Fig. 44). Collars, a comparatively new idea, rose at the back to conceal the cravat, sleeves were so tight that they gave to the fashionable wearer the look of a child growing out of his clothes—and long lace ruffles reaching to the knuckles filled the gap at wrist which would otherwise occur when the arm was bent.

FIG. 43

This effect of too tight clothes was accentuated by the gradual lenghtening of the breeches (see Fig. 43). Almost skin-tight they reached some four or five inches below the knee where a bright buckle fastened them. Stockings with stripes began to be the rage, striped waistcoats too. The hairdressing rose in style to compete to a certain extent with the ladies' growing height, but this fashion was comparatively short-lived and its natural discomfort and an inability to wear a hat curtailed what might otherwise have been a prolonged fashion. Certain dashing young men carrying the style to excess wore absurdly minute tricorn hats perched on their high wigs—and excessively high heels. They were referred to as 'Macaronis', after the Italian fashion, rather than the fops of an earlier generation. Long coats and cloaks were worn more often than they had been as the coats were so abbreviated, and the caped 'Coachman's Coat' first appeared during the 'seventies.

Again referring to Hogarth we find in his drawing the best possible collection of wigs worn at the Coronation of George III in 1760. These are

94

1750   1775

FIG. 44

illustrated here so that comparisons can be drawn between 1726 and 1760 (Fig. 45).

From the Prologue 'Bon Ton', by George Colman 1775, wigs are given their proper names. . . .

> '. . . Tyburn Scratch, Thick Club, Temple Tye.
> The Parson's Feather Top, frizzed broad and High,
> The Coachman's Cauliflower, built tier on tier,
> Differ not more from bags and Brigadiers. . . .'

Horace Walpole's superb cattiness and Boswell's youthful poverty give us almost parallel comments on two sections of the public at the same time. Boswell, dressing for a rout in 1762, said, 'Fain would I had got rich laced clothes,

95

FIG. 45. Wigs, 1760

but I commanded my inclination and got a plain suit of pink colour with gold buttons.' He came home in the evening and put on old clothes, his nightcap and slippers; he bought a pair of lace ruffles which came to sixteen shillings. Then, his pocket being pinched, he cast his eye on an old laced hat and sold the lace for six shillings and sixpence. He sold an old suit of clothes for eleven shillings. He did not hesitate when cold to put on two pairs of woollen stockings, two shirts and a greatcoat. He admired a civil nymph in white thread stockings who tramped along the Strand and when he wanted to appear inconspicuous he described himself thus:

'I dressed myself in my second morning suit in which I had been powdered for months, dirty buckskin breeches and black stockings, a shirt of Lord Eglington's which I had worn two days; a little round hat with tarnished silver lace ... And I was a complete blackguard.'

Of undress one finds that almost anything simple is a relief from the coats and waistcoats and powdered wigs. A friend of Walpole's dined privately in his own dressing-room, putting on a sailor's habit and a black wig. For this early date, 1762, there exists no authentic record of what a sailor's dress was— probably something loose and shapeless like the slops that were issued twenty years later. The black wig, however, was essentially a useful kind, being cheaper and cleaner than a powdered confection, and much adopted by those who didn't care for the nightcaps and turbans that were generally fashionable.

Good clothes were expensive and there are countless records of thefts of clothes, for a decent price could always be had for anything well cut and extravagantly trimmed. In 1765 Walpole lost a portmanteau. ... 'At Chantilly I lost my portmanteau with half my linen; and the night before last I was robbed of a new frock, waistcoat and breeches, laced with gold, a white and silver waistcoat, black velvet breeches, a knife and a book.'

Walpole in 1756, making caustic remarks about Lady Mary Wortley Montague, shows us a degree of tawdriness that must obviously have been a feature of many carelessly dressed persons of that time.

'Do but figure her; her dress had all the tawdry poverty and frippery with which you remember her, and I dare swear her tympany, scarce covered with ticking, produced itself through the slit of her scowered damask robe.'

97

FIG. 46. Waterman, huntsman and pedlar, 1760–1770

The tympany was obviously the heavy wire rather like watchspring wire that supported the drum-like structure of her hip-hoops or panniers. The ticking does not in this case describe the striped bed-ticking with which we are familiar, it was an amazing material full of bounce and made from horsehair; so that it bowed out from the wire supports in a series of springy bulges. (See Fig. 38B, page 82.) Scouring clothes, here referred to, seems to have been the more usual method of cleaning although there is an extremely interesting selection of methods with every possible detail given in a book published in 1758 *Diction-arium Polygraphicum: or the Whole Body of Arts Regularly Digested.* Interesting extracts from this will be found at the end of this book.

Horace Walpole's next catty entry in 1761 runs as follows:

'. . . old Effingham and a Lady Say and Seale, with her hair powdered and her tresses black, were an excellent contrast to the handsome. Lord B. put on rouge upon his wife and the Duchess of Bedford in the Painted Chamber; the Duchess of Queensbury told me of the latter, that she looked like an orange-peach, half red and half yellow. The coronets of the peers and their robes disguised them strangely; it required all the beauty of the Dukes of Richmond and Marlborough to make them noticed. One there was, though of another species, the noblest figure I ever saw, the high constable of Scotland, Lord Errol; as one saw him in a space capable of containing him, one admired him. At the wedding, dressed in tissue, he looked like one of the Giants in Guildhall new gilt. . . .'

This reference to the hair being powdered and the tresses black is singular. I cannot recollect having seen a portrait of anyone with this harlequin effect. Though obviously when Pepys mentions his wife wearing the very blond tresses, 'almost white', the same inspiration is inferred. Whether the reference to the orange peach, half red, half yellow, means the Duchess of Bedford's natural complexion was yellow, or that the make-up was in two colours, is a doubtful point. Though according to portraits of this time the rouge is definitely very pink. Lord Errol looking like the 'giant in Guildhall, new gilt' is not at all far fetched when one sees the amazing effect of gold tissue which is still in perfect condition on many of the eighteenth century coats and gowns in existence today.

In 1762 he made another sly dig at the fashions:

'It will be warmer, I hope, by the King's birthday, or the old ladies will catch their deaths. There is a court dress to be instituted (to thin the drawing-rooms)

—stiff-bodied gowns and bare shoulders. What dreadful discoveries will be made both on fat and lean.'

Twenty years earlier he remarked how ridiculous it was to see old ladies

'who for having been wives of patriots have not been dressed these twenty years. Out they come in all their accoutrements that were in use in Queen Anne's days. I met several on the birthday and they were dressed in all colours of the rainbow. They seem to have said to themselves twenty-three years ago "Well, if ever I go to Court again I will have pink and silver, or blue and silver".....'

It was also in 1762 that he had the grace to mention Lady Mary Wortley without being quite so rude.

'Lady Mary Wortley too was there, dressed in yellow velvet and sables, with a decent laced head and a black hood, almost like a veil, over her face. She is much more descreet than I expected, and meddles with nothing—but she is woefully tedious in her narrations.'

It was towards the end of the 'fifties that the really fashionable began to discard their hoops except for full dress. The hoops as worn until about 'fifty-five were unusually large and had developed into the panniers or side hoops that

Fig. 47.   Typical back view of gown, 1750

not only complicated movement and sitting down, but also made an amusing sight in a strong wind, and seemed to have provoked several artists to indulge in the funny as well as the decorative sights they saw. Paul Sandby's drawings are perhaps the most delightful of this period and show the vivid contrast between static dignity and the ludicrous effect when battling with a wind or sitting down without sufficient practice (see Chapter heading).

In 'fifty-four Mrs. Delany writes to her daughter about the fashions.

'Yesterday after chapel the Duchess brought home Lady Coventry to feast me, and a feast she was! She is a fine figure and vastly handsome, notwithstanding a silly look sometimes about her mouth; she has a thousand airs, but with a sort of innocence that diverts one. Her dress was a black silk sack, made for a large hoop, which *she wore without any, and it trailed a yard on the ground*; she had on a cobweb laced handkerchief, a pink satin long cloke, lined with ermine, mixed with squirrel skins; on her head a French cap that just covered the top of her head, of blond, and stood in the form of a butterfly with its wings not quite extended, frilled sort of lappets crossed under her chin, and tied with pink and green ribbon—a head-dress that would have charmed a *shepherd*! She has a thousand dimples and prettiness in her cheeks, her eyes a little drooping at the corners, but fine for all that; . . .'

This is one of the earliest entries regarding the hoops being left off in England and an amusing sight it must have provoked, for skirts had been made with pleated sides to hang from the enormous hoops. I have drawn one from an existing gown to show the effect, which could be quite a useful one on the stage (see Fig. 48). In 'fifty-five the same correspondent writes on January 15th, 'All I can learn of fashions is that peoples heads are dressed much as they were last year, hoops only worn when full dressed and those large.'

This, of course, does not mean that immediately the fashions changed the gown also changed; there would have been many people who still retained the hoops for informal wear, but it does give us a definite clue to the date of many gowns made during the eighteenth century for 'morning' wear that are uniformly short and were not built out at the sides to take the hoops. The majority of sacks were certainly made for hoops because they were more often than not used for full dress. The full dress type would have a longer back to train.

FIG. 48

FIG. 49

FIG. 50

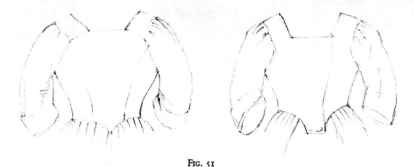

FIG. 51

Although the hoops were no longer fashionable, the quilted petticoat still did quite a lot to keep the skirts out from the hips. Most of these are between three and a half and four yards round the bottom, and the entire width is gathered into the tapes at the waist.

The handkerchief, fischu or little cape was nearly always worn in the day-time during the 'fifties (see Figs. 48 and 50), a few years later the gown again appears with its square neck-line visible, sometimes with a twisted lace kerchief (see Fig. 39) which was known as a neck lace.

The simpler gowns were made with much less skirt (see Fig. 51)—the bodice meeting or crossing in front, but the skirt being pleated back three or four inches to the sides so that the petticoat showed much more than it had done in the past, and a much larger apron was required to cover this.

Full dress and sacks were still made with a petticoat of the same material, and the same fashion for cutting the fronts of the skirts away towards the bottom began to creep into women's dress as well as men's.

A comparatively simple style of dress came into use during the 'sixties, a breath of light and air before the oncoming storm of decoration and head-dressing that, commencing in the 'seventies, practically extinguished any feminine charm by its overloading during the following 15 or 20 years.

The 'sixties undoubtedly held a pastoral charm of their own, in no way linked with the so-called pastoral of Marie Antoinette.

The immediate and understandable effect of being without hoops was one of new-found grace—this was to a certain extent enhanced by the need to tuck

FIG. 52. 1772

up skirts that were too long, and a variety of tucked-up and bunched effects appeared—rather more casual than intentional (see Fig. 52 and tail-piece). Tapes were sewn inside the skirts so that these tucked-up arrangements could be controlled. Buttons on the outside and loops inside helped to hitch up a long gown when necessary.

The fronts of the skirt were also sometimes pulled up through the 'pocket' slits at the sides. The contrast in full dress with the latest device in hinged hip-hoops so that an even more unwieldy skirt could be moved, must have been very noticeable, and the flattened effect lent itself readily to the newest forms of decoration which were pleating, rouching, and a variety of ornaments often made from the self material of the gown. The craze for gigantic patterns and embroideries had died down quite early in the 'fifties. In fact, there are fewer hand-embroidered gowns after 1760 than there are men's coats and waistcoats. The imported Chinese, Italian, and French silks and paduasoys were being furiously competed against in Spitalfield market, and the taxes on imported materials were becoming increasingly high so that we find a genuine new interest in the home-woven fabrics. Many of these, following the pastoral theme, were woven with alternate stripes and bunches of flowers. Plaids and small realistic designs of flowers, fruit, and feathers were quickly replacing the larger patterns that had been such a help to cover the gigantic area of a hooped petticoat. Striped and shot taffetas and watered silks were also much in use. Even the Court dresses changed quite suddenly during the 'fifties; instead of the exotic and colourful displays at balls, Court functions and Birthdays which must have resembled a florist's shop, we find a new-found dignity in white, gold, and silver, and a great deal of jewellery.

The following descriptions by different hands all tend to comment on this new fashion.

> 1754. 'Our Duchess and Lady Betty came to town on Thursday, and we have been very full of business in settling the jewels and clothes for the Birthday. The Duchess of Portland's is white and silver ground, flowered with gold and silver, and a stomacher of white satin, covered with her fine *coloured* jewels, and *all* her diamonds. Lady Betty is to have a very fine sprig of pearl, diamonds and turquoises for her hair, by way of pompome, loops and stars of diamonds between on blue satin for her stomacher; her clothes white and silver, mosaic ground

flowered with silver, intermixed with a little blue. She rehearsed her clothes and jewels yesterday, and practised dancing with her train, she looks mighty well, and is a very genteel figure.'

1757. 'The Duchess, who looks and is extremely well, was in blue and silver flowered velvet; Lady Harriet in rose-coloured and silver velvet; and Lady Betty in white and silver. Hardly anything but silver to be seen; the young ladies had all the Duchess's fine jewels besides their own, and looked and danced remarkably well.'

1759. 'My Lady Coventry showed George Selwyn her clothes; they are blue, with spots of silver, of the size of a shilling, and a silver trimming, and cost— my lord will know what. She asked George how he liked them; he replied, "Why, you will be change for a guinea." '

That stays still retained a rather flattened and wide effect is obvious from contemporary disparaging references. *The World* of 1753 records a letter from a discouraged gentleman bewailing the necessity for such garments.

'The worst reason for coming to London I have ever heard of in my life was given to me last night by a young lady of the most graceful figure I have ever beheld; it was "to have her shape altered to the modern fashion". That is to say to have her breasts compressed by a flat straight line, which is to extend crosswise from shoulder to shoulder and also to descend, still in a straight line, in such a manner as you shall not be able to pronounce what it is that prevents the usual tapering of the waist. I protest when I saw the beautiful figure that was to be so deformed by a stay-maker. I could not help reciting those once-admired lines in the Henry and Emma—

> "No longer shall the bodice aptly laced,
> From thy full bosom to thy slender waist,
> That air of harmony, of shape expressed
> Fine by degrees, and beautifully less—
> An horseman's coat shall hide
> Thy taper shape and comliness of side." '

It is always confusing to follow the immediate fashions and the contemporary names they are given, and from time to time one is confronted with

FIG. 53

descriptions and names of garments which are quite contrary to one's expectations. Apparently even in the eighteenth century the same 'fashion notes' were confusing. In 1755 Mrs. Delaney wrote to her daughter the following double confusion—for surely even at this date a 'Pompadour' must have meant what it does today and certainly not a 'pelisse' (which in Victorian times was not a hooded cloak).

> . . . 'I don't know what you mean by a "Pompadour", unless it is what we call in this part of the world a "Pelisse", which in plain English is a long cloak made of satin or velvet, black or any colour, lined or trimmed with silk, satin, or fur according to the fancy, with slits for the arms to come out and a head like a "capachins"! They are worn by everybody, they come down half-way the petticoat.' (Similar in cut to Fig. 65.)

There are a number of such 'Pelisses' in museums still, often enchantingly lined with a brilliant coloured silk and a thin woollen or even 'down' interlining. Beautifully warm yet as light as a feather and made from the finest silks, they obviously were the most suitable garment to wear over a 'sack'.

The fitted coats (see Figs. 53A, B and C) were still cut on similar lines to the men's coats, with and without 'capachins', but these could only be worn with a fitted gown and petticoat. Padded and quilted coats and petticoats were worn both indoors, in cold weather, and for pillion riding and travelling. The illustrated suit (see Fig. 54), in cream silk with a linen lining and swansdown interlining, is a magnificent specimen of fine quilting and was probably made as a visiting suit. The waistcoat front to the coat is sewn in so that the suit is definitely a coat and petticoat only and did not require a gown underneath. The trill at the elbow and the collar and cut away skirt are definite indications of its date—some time in the 'fifties. Earlier than 1750 the normal finish to a sleeve was the cuff, but later than 1750 the accent was on the frilling and the ruffles that showed beneath. It is also unusual to find a collar or definite revers on any coat earlier than this date.

Warmth was a primary consideration—even if the materials used often appear so flimsy in comparison with our modern ones. Linings and interlining were used for practically all garments and still a considerable amount of fur—to judge by descriptions.

Directions about mourning are, at this time, very odd. Apparently 'grey'

FIG. 54. Quilted travelling suit, c. 1750

was considered a deeper mourning than black, and the following three entries taken again from Mrs. Delany's letters are extremely interesting.

1747. 'I think black bombazeen will do very well in a sack. I have one in a manteau and petticoat which I wear when in full dress, at home a dark grey poplin, and abroad, undrest, a dark grey unwatered tabby: I shall make no more dark things; after three months black silk is worn with love hood, and black glazed gloves, for three months more; your mourning must be the same for Mr. Dewes of Mapleborough.'

1758. 'About mourning: bombazeens quite plain, broad-hemmed muslin, or *white* crape, that looks like old flannell, seven shillings a yard, and won't wash; Turkey gauze is also worn, which is thick and white, but is extravagant, as it does not wash, dirties in two days and cost 5s. a yard; the mourning will be worn *six months*, three in crape and bombazeen.'

1759. 'I think Mary will become a robe very much; but if the mourning is to be the same as for Princess Caroline, she must lay her costly robes aside for some time, and dress like other girls of her age. For second mourning, if she is in town, a white satin may do as well as pink; but I believe the deep mourning will last till April.'

The Countess Cowper writing in 1768 of the wedding of one of her household used the word nightgown as a morning gown and the following rather confusing entry occurs.

'This morning Godwin was married at nine o'clock at Richmond Church. She had a new white satin nightgown and petticoat, a white spotted satin cloak, and bonnet trimmed with blond, new lace handkerchief and ruffles upon gauze, a clear apron, and I gave her a very handsome pair of stone shoe-buckles. After they were married they came here, and I ordered that breakfast should be ready for them in the steward's room.'

This description (apart from the cloak) exactly describes the painting of 'Pamela's Wedding' by Highmore, now in the Victoria and Albert Museum, although the painting is probably several years earlier than the description.

Repeatedly we find the use of the words nightgown, undress, morning dress, sultane—all of which mean a tight-fitting bodice with a full skirt, the bodice of the gown fastening right across or doing up with buttons and loops

III

FIG. 55

(as the sultane invariably does), no stomacher being visible, and no petticoat to match. A quilted petticoat and a long apron would usually be worn with this undress.

Hairdressing styles underwent several drastic changes between 1750 and 1775. For the first few years the hair was dressed in rolls and curls—powdered and covered with a cap or some tiny decoration very similar in style to the matrons' caps that again appeared in the 'fifties and 'sixties of the nineteenth century.

During the 'sixties the style began to rise. Little pads and rolls were put on top of the head and the hair was dressed over this; bonnets naturally had to be of a different shape and they tended to get larger with a deeper frill at the sides, making the face oval rather than round. By about 'sixty-five there is a very definite rise—the beginning of the high hairdressing, and the tall wig was on its way (Fig. 56).

FIG. 56

For the first year or two of the high hairdressing, hats were abandoned altogether and caps and hoods, or capuchins, were the only form of covering. As the hairdressing slowly rose in height, it became increasingly insecure; so that some sort of wire construction on the head itself was absolutely necessary. Once this framework had been introduced, hairdressing became a very much more lengthy process; and, when once raised to its full height and false curls and locks attached pomaded and powdered, it became a natural economy to cover it up with care, to reserve it for another night, and for this purpose the calash was invented (see Fig. 63). The calash was a huge frame supported on cane

113

hoops, rather like the hood to a covered waggon, so that it could be folded up and put away flat when not being used. These were worn all day, if my lady went out, and usually at night to protect the erection of hair and powder, wire and pins, from damage. It must be remembered that these fantastic hair styles were not worn by ordinary people; it was very much a Court fashion for ladies of quality and leisure. The average housewife would probably pile her hair up as high as was conveniently practical and wear over it a lace bonnet that tied under her chin, to help to keep it tidy. Although powder was used extensively, it was not universal. There were still women who preferred to show their hair in its natural colour. Absurdly large hats and bonnets rather like inverted lampshades were introduced during the 'seventies and probably reached their most fantastic dimensions in the closing years of the 'eighties. Whether they really helped to keep the hair in place or increased the difficulty of balance is a debatable point.

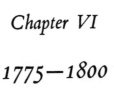

Chapter VI

1775—1800

TWO distinct phases in fashion existed in the last quarter of the eighteenth century, as distinct as the change established in Queen Anne's time. The century can roughly be divided into three—the first ten years, the middle eighty, and the last ten years. The Revolution in France certainly had much to do with the sobering-up process, and men who might well have been sworn enemies of the Directoire and what it stood for found their new military uniforms, darker clothes, boots and a shorter haircut far more comfortable and useful than the fashion of a decade earlier.

As we approach the end of the century there appears a greater difference between the rich and the poor—a sordid shoddiness on one side even more definite than Hogarth's illustrations of an earlier age, and a complacent baby-faced stupidity with an over-fed and over-dressed effect on the other.

The calculated elegance of the late 'seventies and early 'eighties depended almost entirely upon a skin-tight effect attained by the men, and an overwhelming superfluity of draperies, floating scarves, lace, ribbon and powder by the women. The latters' eventual shrinkage took place some twenty years later. Women towered and billowed, whilst men minced and strutted, and contemporary criticism was pretty brutal in its caricature of both.

The traditional eighteenth-century coat had, by 1775, shrunk to the extent of being little more than a covering for back and arms. The fronts were so scanty that a waistcoat must be worn on all occasions and therefore on these vests were lavished the most precious embroideries and delicate handiwork. Existing examples of these elegant garments are in a variety of materials from the fine cut velvets with silk embroidered stripes to the most fragile of silks and satins with beautiful floral embroideries. The latter probably represented gifts from wives and lady friends, as did the dream waistcoat recorded in the tragi-comedy of the present from the Countess of Ossory to Horace Walpole, January 1775.

Arlington St. Jan. 1, 1775

To the Countess of Ossory.

This morning, Madam, as soon as my eyes opened, Philip (his servant) stood before me, bearing in one hand a shining vest, and in the other a fair epistle, written in celestial characters, which, however, it was given me to understand.

The present, I saw, came from no mortal hand, and seemed to be the boon of all the gods, or rather of all the goddesses; for there was taste, delicacy, flattery, wit, and sentiment in it, and so artfully blended, that no celestial in breeches could possibly have mixed so bewitching a potion. Venus had chosen the pattern, Flora painted the roses after those at Paphos, Minerva had worked the tambour part, Clio wrote the ode, and Thalia took off the majestic stiffness of the original sketch by breathing her own ease all over it.

These visions naturally presented themselves. I told you, Madam, I was but just awake, and at that hour, somehow or other, one's head is very apt to be full of Venus and such pretty figures. Vanity soon took their place, and, not to be unworthy of my visitants, I held up my head, and thought it became so favoured a personage as myself to assume a loftier port, and behave like my predecessors who had been honoured in the same manner.

Was I more like Aeneas when his mother brought him armour of heavenly temper, or like Paris, when three divinities exerted all their charms and all their artifices to ensnare his partiality? To be sure I could have been simple enough to be content with the character of Horatius Flaccus, with which my patronesses had hailed me; but when I ordered Philip to reach me my lyre, that I might pour out a rapturous ode or secular hymn in gratitude, he said, "Lord! sir, you know Horace's lyre is at Ampthill."

What follows is more melancholy. I rose; the first object was to examine more attentively the inspired vest in the full sun against which it shone gorgeously; but, alas! as I crept to the window, in the glass I beheld—what do you think, Madam?—such an emaciated, wan, wrinkled, poor skeleton, that—O! adieu, visions, goddesses, odes, vests of roses, and immortal Strawberry!—I thought I saw a thinner Don Quixote attired by the Duchess for sport. Shocked,

116

sunk from my altitudes, and shrinking into myself, I bade Philip Panca fold up
the vest, and vowed never to dress up my ghost-like Adonis, but to consecrate
the dear work of dear fingers to the single word (I will believe in the charming
ode) Friendship; and may the memory of that word, the vest and the ode, exist
when Strawberry Hill, its tinsel glories and its master, are remembered no where
else!

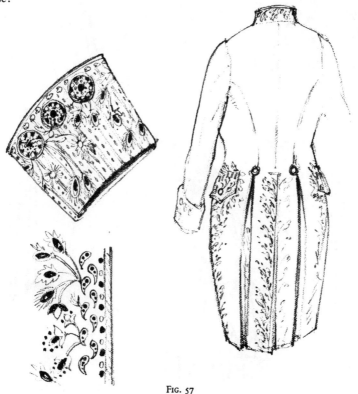

FIG. 57

Men's Court clothes had stepped beyond the bounds of embroidered
beauty and plunged into an orgy of glittering decoration. Jewels, glass, little
mirrors, sequins, gold and silver ornaments worth a fortune, flashed and glowed
in the light from a thousand candles (see Fig. 57). Gold and silver tissue stiffened

FIG. 58. The fashionable coat was made so that it must stick out at the back, rather like a beetle's wings. Every scrap of fullness was contained in the back pleats. The sleeves were practically skin tight and rather short

with embroideries vied in splendour with the most exquisite cut velvets, cut in a bewildering number of enchanting designs and picked out with spots of colour or sequins. Court dress for men became stabilised some time during the 'seventies, and a formal acceptance of colourful sloped coats, knee-breeches, embroidered waistcoats, white wigs, silk stockings and shoes with buckles prevailed until the end of the century. This, however, was not the case in France, for after the Revolution, when there was no longer a Court, formal and ceremonial attire was black, and for some reason this same black formal suit crept into England at George IV's Court.

The everyday clothes, both informal and utilitarian, were at long last beginning to change. Between 1775 and 1780 the last of the Macaronis were seen (see Fig. 58). Wigs—swept up over a high frontal pad and those raised all over like a very large egg in a small egg-cup—vanished with a rather abrupt suddenness, and for a few years a fairly natural effect was achieved with side curls or a bob or Tye wig. The 'Treasonable Cut' of natural hair cut really short appeared in France in the early days of the Revolution, but a definite stigma was attached to it in England for some time and the nearest approach to this fashion was the ear length cut which began to be seen in the late 'eighties, a natural attempt at the effect of a bob wig. German styles remained rather exotic with many rolls and loops, and doubled up tails, but the Englishman was beginning to prefer his own hair.

Long trousers, or pantaloons as they were first called, had been worn by little boys several years before they were worn generally—they also appear to have been worn by sailors and workmen some ten or fifteen years earlier; but by 1793 the knee-breeches had become so elongated that the pantaloons had arrived (see Fig. 59). Late in the 'eighties boots were worn, and before the end of the century boots were more fashionable than shoes and were made in a dozen different styles, from the elegant drawing room affair to the hearty Wellington or Hessian in its earliest form.

There are curious glimpses of striped and patterned stocking that appear between the top of the boot and the breeches.

Hardly an article of men's clothing retained its shape during the 'nineties, and although the 'frock' coat was still cherished for many years in country districts, the newer shapes predominated.

New experiments in coats introduced the double-breasted, the cut-away and the first tail coat during the 'eighties (see Figs. 59 and 61).

Buttons and buttonholes, which served no functional purpose other than decoration, appear on all these coats; sometimes there are two sets of buttons,

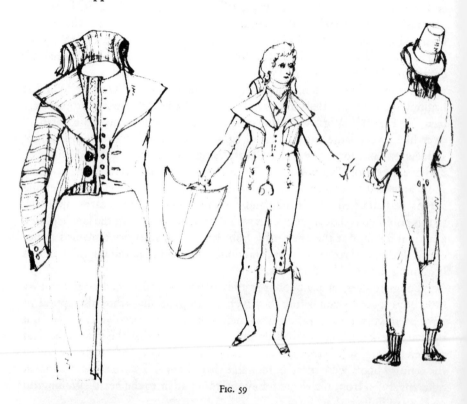

FIG. 59

one each side. Frogs, braid and tassels all helped to trim these narrow fronts. Collars steadily rose in height, and assumed more importance as the century drew towards its close. This fashion was governed to a certain extent by the use of wigs. As the wig ceased to take up so much attention, and the fashion for wearing one's own hair began to be popular with the younger generation

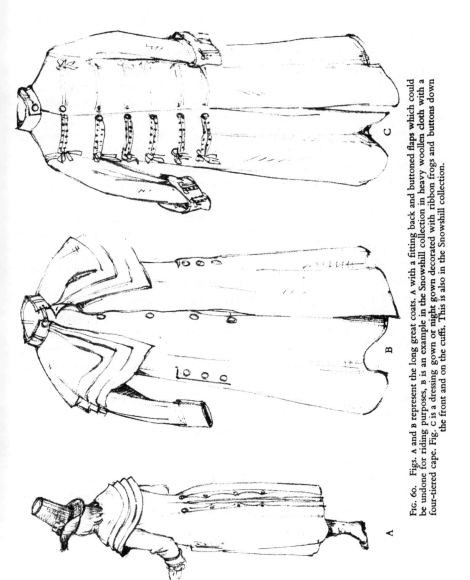

Fig. 60. Figs. A and B represent the long great coats. A with a fitting back and buttoned flaps which could be undone for riding purposes, B is an example in the Snowshill collection in heavy woollen cloth with a four-tiered cape. Fig. C is a dressing gown or night gown decorated with ribbon frogs and buttons down the front and on the cuffs. This is also in the Snowshill collection.

the collar rose, climbing eventually to the ears, and covering the back of the neck (see Fig. 59).

The variety in clothes was such that no two men in a group of a dozen need be wearing a similar outfit—this must have been, after the conformity of the last sixty years, rather an interesting spectacle. The change from the almost traditional tricorn was in itself surprising and hatters seemed to vie with one another to produce something new and unusual; but before the close of the century the top-hat in its earliest form (see Fig. 59) had replaced the tricorn and the latter gradually descended in its social scale until it became the accepted headgear of coachmen and footmen and the elderly and unfashionable.

The long great-coat (see Fig. 60) was much in evidence during the last quarter of the century, probably because the newer coats were so much briefer. The sharply sloping fronts with buttons that were never intended to do up must have been as chilly as the new short-waisted cut-away variety, the fashion for short waistcoats also left the legs exposed. To a certain extent the growing use of buckskin for pantaloons was probably as a protection from the cold as much as to achieve a fashionable skin fitting outline.

There are still quite a number of these pantaloons in existence in spite of the fact that a pair made in 1790 could have been worn for about 30 years—they were dyed in a variety of colours as well as being worn in the natural buff, nearly always laced below the knee and at the back of the waist. The front was always fastened with a front flap very much the same as a sailor's bell-bottoms today.

An account of Paris fashions in September and October 1798 includes a reference to flesh-coloured pantaloons as well as the following interesting notes of the disappearance of Revolutionary uniformity.

'The barbel-blue colour of men's coats is not now so generally adopted. We see much iron grey, and horn, beside the black, which is always in great vogue; a black coat is not now used for ceremony, as we see them worn with boots or pantaloons. The boots, very pointed at the toes, do not reach higher than the calf of the leg. They are highly polished, which is the way in which our young people shine. The pantaloons, generally of nankeen, reach within two inches of the ankle, where it is tied with a ribband forming a small rose. The breeches, less tight, are more decent than before. The waistcoat is edged with black. Two small round flaps are formed into a kind of heart at the bottom.'

The bright colours and embroideries had quite disappeared for ordinary wear. Greys, browns, dark blue and bottle green appeared in all stuff coats, the

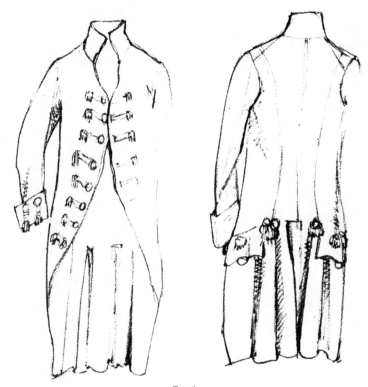

FIG. 61

waistcoat, more often striped than plain, was the last bright gesture of the eighteenth century.

The shape of the shirt had been maintained right through the century, even to the ruffle down the front which was first mentioned during the early years of

FIG. 62

Queen Anne's reign. The cravat had seen many changes and its formal arrangement during the last years of the century was due to the high collar on the coat.

The extravagant head-dress of the 'seventies was undoubtedly influenced by French example. Where a powdered and piled-up head of hair was charming in England, the French made it fantastic with wires, postiches, false curls and ornaments of exotic and orchidaceous flavour. By 1775 the owner of a good head of hair was rarely to be envied, for no one, not even her nearest and dearest, could say if others less fortunately endowed wore their own hair. The fashion for powdering had very gradually gained a hold, but where in the 'forties it had been a mere lightening of the head to set off jewels or 'pompoms', it was now a heavily larded and powdered confection hardly recognisable as a head of hair—a superstructure to support such trimmings as might appeal to a hairdresser with a sense of humour. Ribbons, lace, feathers, and flowers were the simplest ornaments, but there are fashion-plates still in existence that show ships and windmills, coaches and horses—the sort of ornaments to adorn a wedding cake or a centre piece for a table. Such things appeared at Balls and Routs, though bonnets were worn in the house—gigantic bonnets tied under the chin to keep the precarious erection under control (see Fig. 63). The fashion for feathers came directly from the French Court, and Horace Walpole, writing in 1775-6, remarked this as an interesting feature:

> 'The vivacity of the young Queen of France has reached hither. Our young ladies are covered with more plumes than any nation that has no other covering.'
> . . . 'You ask, what is become of the Duchess of Kingston? I have just heard of her, having met Lady Harriet Vernon, who is returned from Paris, and saw her there at the Colisee, with a hat and feathers like Henri Quatre.'

It was, however, several years later that the real feather mania set in and fashion-plates of the 'nineties are rarely devoid of feathers.

Although the hairdressing of the 'seventies was fantastically high and frequently absurd, there was a certain dignity and charm about it which was both amusing and, in a great many instances, most attractive. The 'eighties, however, held little of this sort of provocation, for it was becoming more and more fashionable to curl, puff, pad, back-comb and powder the natural hair out all

FIG. 63

round the face with curls, '*à la négligence*', hanging all round the shoulders and down the back. This thick 'woolly' effect was frequently recorded by such artists as Gainsborough, Lawrence and Reynolds. Although the effect aimed at was one of simplicity and naturalness, there is nothing simple or natural in the result. In 1786, when Fanny Burney was lady-in-waiting to Queen Charlotte, she recorded the following rigmarole about her hairdressing problems:

'My next difficulty was for a hair-dresser. Nuneham is 3 or 4 miles from Oxford; and I had neither maid to dress, nor man to seek a dresser. I could only apply to Mrs. Thielky, and she made it her business to prevail with one of the royal footmen to get me a messenger, to order a hair-dresser from Oxford at 6 o'clock in the morning. The Queen, with most gracious consideration, told me, over-night, that she should not want me till eight o'clock. Aug. 13. At 6 o'clock my hair-dresser, to my great satisfaction arrived. Full two hours was he at work, yet was I not finished when Swarthy, the Queen's hair-dresser, came rapping at my door, to tell me Her Majesty's hair was done and she was waiting for me. I hurried as fast as I could and ran down without any cap. . . . When her Majesty was dressed, all but the hat, she sent for the three Princesses; and the King came also. I felt very foolish with my uncovered head; but it was somewhat the less awkward from its being very much a custom, in the Royal Family, to go without caps; though none that appear before them use such a freedom.'

Fashion notes for 1790 include the following description of hair and head-dress in the *Lady's Magazine*:

'*Head-dresses.* The caps most worn were very high and narrow, chiefly of white and coloured crapes suitable to the dresses, and richly trimmed with blond lace. The ornaments were ostrich and vulture feathers, and many ladies wore white beads. Portes Plumes were worn in a few head-dresses. They are a pretty ornament of steel or brilliants to hold the feathers.
The Hair was dressed with great neatness, neither preposterously large nor too small. The toupee was in curls off the sides, with two drop curls.'

Gradually the head is becoming smaller, though feathers were absurdly large. In December 1795 *The Times* noted:

'The Ladies now wear feathers exactly of their own length, so that a woman of fashion is twice as long upon her feet as in her bed'.

During the same year caps were discarded for Court wear and in 'ninety-eight powder was no longer worn. The following year the first record of short hair appeared in the *Lady's Magazine*.

'*Fashions of Paris—September.*
Since the change of female head-dresses, hats have also assumed a new form. The fore and hind parts are not so large in the brim as the sides, and are absolutely turned down, while the sides are turned up, and as it were curled. Perhaps we owe this variation to the hatters, *who perceived all the deformity which the cropt heads would present*, if the hind part of the hat was turned up as before. It is a sign of good taste to correct those defects which characterise the inventions of caprice.

Nobody takes off the hat as heretofore. The point of support is the nape of the neck; thence it is drawn up to the crown of the head, taking care not to disorder the hair. The manner of wearing them is also quite different. They are placed almost in the same way as leather caps and the forehead is only shaded by the hair.'

About 1775 there appeared a new gown, probably a derivation of the sack but without its great pleats. This was worn first in France (illustrated on Chapter heading). The back, cut with a square or oval neckline, had three long seams which held the shape from shoulder to a few inches below the waist, where added fullness swept out in a flared line to be gathered up into a slight bustle effect half-way to the bottom of the petticoat. Such gowns were often used as undress or morning wear; they could easily be worn as a coat, hanging open in front with no fastenings and falling away from the body at the back. Petticoats were getting increasingly short, the ankles and several inches of leg quite often being seen. Indeed many of the porcelain figures of this time are wearing petticoats not much below the calf, and very high heels (Fig. 64).

There is still a certain charm in the fashions of the late 'seventies although the high hairdressing and short skirt gave a slightly unbalanced effect—especially with full dress when great hoops supported an abundance of decoration—pleating, jewels, drapery and great bunches of flowers—but as long as the waist-line was slightly longer than normal the effect could be delightful with a full-length petticoat.

That quilted petticoats survived until the 'eighties as a necessary padding to a dress is recorded in an amusing entry about an infamous young lady named

FIG. 64.   Underwear, 1780

Bet Flint. This also gives us an idea of the uses to which a quilt could be put:

'. . . She stole a quilt from a man of the house, and he had her taken up; but Bet Flint had a spirit not to be subdued; so when she found herself obliged to go to jail, she ordered a sedan chair and bid her footboy walk before her . . . when she came to her trial the judge acquitted her. "So now," she said to me, "the quilt is my own, and now I'll make a petticoat of it." '

There are frequent references to jackets and coats and even bed-gowns that might all easily have been the same or similar garments. It must therefore be remembered still that the prefix 'bed', 'night', and even 'morning' means a house-dress rather than a travelling or formal gown—it was not necessarily slept in.

Mrs. Thrale wrote in 1782:

'I had a very pretty sort of a bed-gown, like a jacket, hanging at the fire, and I had on a petticoat, with a border on it of the same pattern; but the bed-gown I thought was damp, and I was in a hurry to go down to Mrs. Ord, so I would not stay to dry it, but went down in another bed-gown, and put my cloak on. But only think what Mrs. Ord must think of it, for I have since thought she must suppose I had no gown on at all, for you must know my cloak was so long it only showed the petticoat.'

Undress at this time seems to have become accepted even for formal occasions, as is shown by a contemporary description of a ball:

'The room was very thin, and almost half the ladies danced with one another, though there were men enough present, I believe, had they chosen such exertion; but the Meadowses at balls are in crowds. Some of the ladies were in riding habits, and they made admirable men. 'Tis *tonnish* to be so much undressed at the last ball.'

Dr. Johnson's few remarks about fashions were always caustic; in 1778 we learn that:

'. . . Mrs. Burney had on a very pretty linen jacket and coat, and was going to church; but Dr. Johnson, who, I suppose, did not like her in a jacket, saw something was the matter and so found fault with the linen; and he looked and

FIG. 65

peered, and then said, "Why, madam, this won't do! you must not go to church so!" So away went poor Mrs. Burney and changed her gown! And when she had done so, he did not like it, but he did not know why; so he told her she should not wear a black hat and cloak in summer!

Last time she came she was in a white cloak, and she told Dr. Johnson she had got her old white cloak scoured on purpose to oblige him! "Scoured!" says he, "ay—have you, madam?"—so he see-sawed, for he could not for shame find fault, but he did not seem to like the scouring.'

One can sympathise with Samuel Johnson's dislike of ladies' fashions in the 'eighties, for it is recorded that he rarely liked anyone in anything considered fashionable. Looking at the drawings of the time this attitude is not to be condemned, for never have ladies' clothes been quite so absurdly complicated and at the same time so unsuitable. Nothing was simple, and an over-abundance of draperies such as scarves and fichus, shawls, kerchiefs, bits of gauze and aprons seemed to be draped everywhere. The hats were like great lamp-shades and the simplest bonnet assumed the proportions of a Mother Hubbard's Panto-mime bonnet. These were draped with bandeaux, scarves, and lace, and trimmed with yards of goffered frills, feathers and other gee-gaws (see Figs. 65 and 67).

There is a series of prints depicting the seasons, originally drawn by R. Dighton about the year 'eighty-five, which gives all the fashionable ensembles which were probably unremarkable at the time, for these are not fashion plates, as they merely illustrated seasonable changes. There is not a dress that is either simple or attractive; each figure looks overloaded, overdressed and almost extinguished by hat and hair, and practically immobilised by the bulk of her clothes and the trailing quality of her garments.

There was also a fashionable air of white-faced fragility which gave the bundled-up effect the sordid quality of a confirmed invalid, or a consumptive, staggering feebly out into the fresh air, well muffled from the chill winds for a last look at nature. This effect was probably much accentuated by the powder from the hair, but cosmetics were used with impunity. In 1779 a young lady of lovely complexion died, apparently from poisoning herself with the use of white lead.

'A new light is of late thrown upon the death of poor Sophy P. Dr. Hervey, of Tooting, who attended her the day before she expired, is of opinion that she

FIG. 66

killed herself by quackery, that is, by cosmetics and preparations of lead or mercury, taken for her complexion, which, indeed, was almost unnaturally white.
He thinks, therefore, that this pernicious stuff got into her veins, and poisoned
her. Pegg P, nearly as white as her sister, is suspected strongly of using the same
beautifying methods of destroying herself; but as Mrs. Thrale has hinted this
suspicion to her, and charged her to take care of herself, we hope she will be
frightened, and warned to her safety. Poor foolish girls! how dearly do they pay
for the ambition of being fairer than their neighbours.'

From 1785 the waistline began to rise, and though at first this new effect
was strictly governed by the wearing of short high stays, which forced the
breasts even higher than they had been before, necessitating the discreet use of
fichus and scarves—these were discarded by the young and fashion loving
public from about 1793 onwards, and the less worn the more elegant was the
effect attempted if not always achieved. We have only to look at Rowlandson's
drawings to see the all too prevalent contours this fashion revealed.

The elderly and more restrained members of society continued to look
bundled up until the end of the century, though their gowns trailed rather
forlornly with an obvious deflated air, and their heads still retained the over-
dressed effect to which they had become accustomed during their youth.

During the late 'eighties, although the dress seemed very different from those
of a few years earlier it was still fundamentally the same (see Fig. 66). The
bodice was still made to fit tightly and fasten in front, the skirt pleated on in
minute pleats from the V at the back and over the hips, with a wide opening in
front to display the shortened petticoat worn underneath. The sleeve as before
was eased on to the shoulder-band and remained fairly tight-fitting to just
below the elbow. The only real difference was that the back was longer, often
trailing some inches on the ground behind and rising in a curved line from there
to the waist in front.

It looked so different because the stays had changed and the breasts were
forced up as high as human elasticity would allow, then the too-revealing curves
were muffled up in a fichu giving an almost deformed pouter pigeon effect (see
Fig. 67). Little coats were worn with flared tails sticking out from the waist
behind, aprons, usually transparent and very large, covered the petticoat in front
and others less transparent and even larger were often worn behind. Sashes,

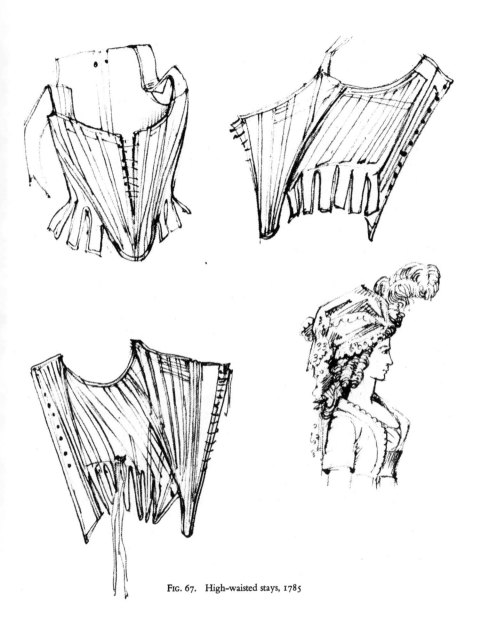

FIG. 67. High-waisted stays, 1785

scarves and kerchiefs and vague bits of gauze and ruffles on the sleeves all helped to disguise a gown that might have been worn thirty or forty years earlier.

'. . . Mr. Crutchley, turning about and looking at Mrs. Davenant, as she came forward said, rather in a muttering voice, and to himself than to me, "What a thing for an attachment! No, no, it would not do for me!—too much glare! too much flippancy! too much hoop! too much gauze! too much slipper! too much neck! Oh, hide it! hide it!—muffle it up! muffle it up! If it is but in a fur cloak, I am for muffling it all up!" '

The waistline was gradually getting higher, particularly in front, for the back was still cut in much the same pleated and tucked manner. The original idea of a centre panel from neck to hem was disappearing in favour of a much fuller back to the skirt which was pleated on to the point of the bodice behind; this gave a bustle effect (compare Figs. 62 and 66).

It was the higher waistline that provoked the introduction of a 'round gown', one that went right round and did not split in the front to show a petticoat. To begin with these gowns were made with the front part of the skirt gathered on to a tape with slits or plackets at the side so that the pockets could still be worn in the old manner. The bodice of the gown was attached at the back as far as the plackets, and the front crossed over the skirt and either laced or fastened in some other manner. (See drawings, Fig. 66.)

This same 'round gown' developed during the 'nineties into a cross-over brassière top, and the skirt in front had a bib or flap at the top to fasten to each shoulder so that the 'waist' could be as high as possible (Fig. 69).

At the King's birthday in 1792 the Queen's dress is described in all its dazzling extravagance—obviously in defiance of the tragedy across the channel.

'Her Majesty upon this occasion, was dressed with more magnificence than we remember to have ever seen her before. The petticoat was of green silk, entirely covered with Brussels point, thrown very fully over it, with a loose drapery of lilac silk, covered also with lace, and drawn up in festoons with large bouquets of diamonds, each bouquet consisting of one large rosette, from which rise bending sprigs in imitation of snowdrops. From each rosette fall two large diamond chains and tassels; and upon each festoon of the drapery is a chain of large diamonds.

At the bottom, a flounce of fine lace, headed with rows of large diamonds. The robe and train white and silver silk, trimmed round with a border of lilac silk covered with lace. The cap blond, with bandeaus, and girdle of diamonds.

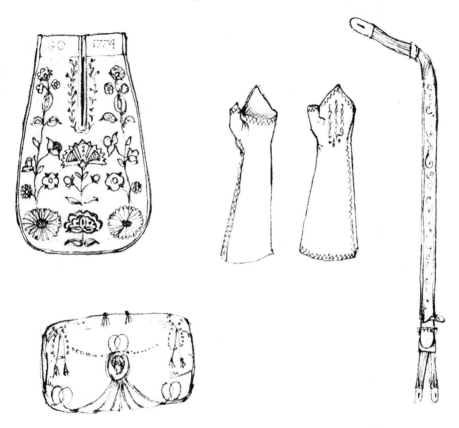

Fig. 68. Embroidered details of pocket, muff, mittens and braces

Each bouquet of the petticoat has a central stone in the rosette valued at £2,000; the rosette, including this stone, is valued at £3,000; and the bouquets, of which there are six, at £8,000 each. Adding to the amount of these that of the other diamonds upon the petticoat, and those upon the head-dress and stomacher, the dress worn by Her Majesty could not be worth less than an hundred thousand pounds; and the taste displayed in the arrangement of the whole was well suited to such an expenditure.'

Undoubtedly the French Revolution had an immediate effect on the fashions of the Western World, and although Court descriptions for Birthdays in England still retain something of their former magnificence, there is a definite lightening in clothes generally. Fabrics are lighter, colours paler, petticoats less, hairdressing not *quite* so fantastic and a spirited attempt to imitate Greek simplicity.

The formal gown had turned into a mere bodice with a skirt at the back only, looking like a train—the petticoat was the more important garment. Such dresses were gradually falling out of fashion to be replaced by the 'round-gown'.

Waists were getting higher and higher, until in 1796 the *Lady's Magazine* reports, 'The waists were so short that ladies had hardly room to move their arms'. However, they went down again in 'ninety-eight and the French fashions for that year are very odd indeed having much the same effect as a Mrs. Noah, having large bosom, tight waist, large hips and again tight at the ankle. Extracts from the *Lady's Magazine* in 1795 include the following rather interesting descriptions:

The Queen's Birthday.
The Caps were, for the most part, in the Turban fashion, made of black and coloured velvet. Several ladies wore turban caps of gold and silver crape, with very high plumes of feathers, which were universally worn.

Several ladies appeared with *tippets* round their necks, of gold and silver laurels, which had a novel and very pretty effect. *The Hair* was dressed in a loose fashion, but much concealed by the caps.

Necklaces and ear-rings of cornelian were chiefly worn; except by those ladies who had diamonds or pearls.

There were not so many new dresses yesterday at court, as we have been accustomed to see; several ladies choosing to reserve theirs for the first appearance of the princess of Wales at court.

Almost one third of the gentlemen yesterday at court were in regimentals.

138

FIG. 69

Elegant oval buttons, beautifully enriched, of various coloured metals, appeared new, and had a pleasing effect.

Fashions for April.

An Evening Dress. The hair dressed in light curls and ringlets. Turban of light blue crape: bandeau of gold foil, set with diamonds and pearls: the rear hair turned up, mixed with the turban, and the ends returned in ringlets. Jacket and petticoat of sprig muslin; four plaits across the petticoat; the jacket turned on the back with lace. Short sleeves. Small handkerchief trimmed with lace. Sash of blue satin ribband. Three string of pearls round the neck. Pearl ear-rings. Blue satin shoes. White gloves. Swan-down muff.

I. Morning Dress. The hair combed into light curls; plain chignon: white bouffants round the head. Bonnet of black velvet, lined with pink satin: the caul of pink satin, spotted with black; the top fastened and crossed in several parts with black velvet ribband, fastened to a button on the top, trimmed with pink ribband, made into a large bow in front and behind. One black ostrich feather in the front. Round gown of chintz, with a narrow flounce. Full cravat round the neck. Black satin short cloak, trimmed with broad lace. Isabella bear-skin tippet and muff. Red Morocco slippers.

II. Morning Dress. The hair in light curls and ringlets; white satin ribband round the head, tied with a bow in the front: bonnet of black velvet, lined with yellow satin ribband, forming a large bow in the front, and behind; one small bow of black ribband on the left side. Petticoat of worked muslin, with a Van-dyke scollop at the bottom. Spencer of dark blue cloth, edged with scarlet Ruff of white lace round the neck. Plain muslin handkerchief. York tan gloves. Purple shoes. Fur muff.

Although these descriptions appear immensely complicated, they were in reality very simple in contrast to the fashions of the 'eighties. The ordinary people indulged in an absolute orgy of plain or spotted muslin relieved perhaps with a coloured sash—even George Morland's country bumpkins are always depicted in spotless white.

Bonnets and caps were, however, more varied than they had been throughout the century. The elderly still clung to their huge bonnets, and the young tried out all the engaging ideas suggested by the first fashion magazines. Dozens of names appear to describe these new bonnets. 'A Cabriolet bonnet', 'Gipsy and Demi-Gipsy', 'A Chinese hat of Bamboo cane, with red chenile'—'The

Minerva hat', 'The Hive Hat'. The latter has the following description in 1799:

> 'Parisian Fashions for June.
>
> The Hive Hat. The crown is of satin, and also the shape or shade which comes over the face; this last is very narrow, and slopes off at the left side, so as to form an obtuse angle at the extremity. Bands of crape across the crown but one generally of a different colour from it. Silk loop, after twisting round the transverse drapery, runs in a double row along the edge of the shape, and at length falls down on the left side, ornamented with two tassels at the ends.
>
> These hats are generally adorned with a wreath of artificial flowers. Gilly-flower, lilac, and daisy, are mostly preferred. These wreaths lay flat on the shape, in such a manner that the flowers hang over and shade part of the face.'

We have now reached a period where fashionable descriptions are becoming too complicated—almost in the modern jargon of an art critic—too obscure for the general public to understand. In reality these descriptions give only the vaguest of ideas of contemporary dress, for comparatively few women followed the immediate styles. Once the changed silhouette had been established dress followed the prescribed outline with the addition of scarf, cloak, bonnet or turban.

Nightcaps still appear with 'Undress', though undress is now remarkably similar to any other. It is the period when most dresses in collections give the first impression of being nightdresses.

However, contemporary comment seems loud in praise of the beautiful Courts and the following note signed 'Beau Nash' gives a sparkling and warm criticism of the full season in London—the closing season of the eighteenth century.

> 'Fashions of the Season. May.
>
> At no time, for these five years past, have we had so gay, or so full a season in the metropolis, as the present. Fashion has not only resumed all its splendour, but it has, from the interval of rest and economy, acquired new taste for the capricious and expensive. Fancy is now racked for novelties of decoration, and dress is daily flying from Greek simplicity into Eastern magnificence. The embroidery of muslins has given a richness to the female robe which is truly

captivating; and, what with the glittering effect of gold and silver, of high plumes, and of diamonds, the ball-room now presents a blaze of ornamented beauty, from which the sober and chaste elegance of last winter must shrink in dismay. No woman, truly loyal to the divinity of fashion, can possibly appear now without feathers and flowers; and though the gentlemen have not yet been brought to the stiff collar, the sword, and the embroidered suit, yet it is somewhat towards the renovation of becoming grandeur, in opposition to the republican Marseilles waistcoat, and the treasonable crop, that the cocked hat has enlarged its dimensions, and sports its gold tassel, button and loop.

This does not arise, I hope, Mr. Editor, from the mere natural versatility of fashion, but is the result of a wise and profound policy in the administration of the mode. It has been a subject of deep regret, that plainness of dress in public assemblies not only countenances the malignant principle of equality, by confounding distinctions, but cherished the sentiment in the mind, reconciles the taste to simplicity and corrects all the notions of dignity and distance which the costume of courts so properly inculcates. Plainness begets familiarity. No noble lord can be a great don in a pair of pantaloons; even if to all his native high blood he has had the advantage of acquiring state and stiffness at Madrid. And how can a lady of the most illustrious descent awe the humble spectator into reverence, if a mere silken fillet binds her hair, and her muslin is permitted to articulate her shape, by floating in light draperies from the zone that encircles her waist? The thing is impossible, sir; for however lofty her brow, the heart will catch infection from a glance, and homage to her rank will be softened by an emotion which, without daring to be love, has some of its sympathies. I know not but half the gallantries which have lately happened, may be ascribed to the simple nature of the female dress. There was an accommodating ease in it which favoured the approaches of rudeness, and a plainness which could not be disordered; while the encumbrances of finery are succours to virtue in the moment of attack, they cannot be laid aside without delay, nor touched without bearing witness. I should not wonder if, among the other mischievous arts of the directory, it should be proved, in a report from the committee of fashion, that they sent forth the seduction of simplicity in dress, both to increase the temptations to sin, and provide for its immunity.

But this is not the only argument for the change which has been recently introduced. What an illustration of the resources of England is the superb style of the present year? Our fêtes, our balls, our assemblies, are not only more numerous than ever, but our dress is more brilliant; and, thus if the state demands sacrifices from the people, the higher orders, with the magnificence which reconciles the heart to their distinction, liberally spread among the arts their wealth, and like the sun, restore to the mass of society the vivifying riches which they originally draw from their toil.

BEAU NASH.'

Appendix

HINTS ON CLEANING

taken from

'Dictionarium Polygraphicum: or the Whole Body of Arts Regularly Digested'
London, C. Hitch and L. Hawes, Paternoster Row. 1758

To take out spots of grease.—Rub them very well two or three times with oil of turpentine, and they will vanish away inconceivably; and then wash again with rectified spirits of wine.

To take out spots of oil or grease out of white or red silk.—Rub the spots well with diluted aqua-fortis, and afterwards with the glair of new-laid eggs; hang it in the sun to dry, and afterwards wash it with fair water, and press it well.

To take spots of pitch, tar, &c. out of cloth.—Rub either common oil, or hog's lard, well into the spots, and let it lie for twenty-four or forty-eight hours; then rub it well with your hands, and wring it, and lastly wash it clean with soap and water.

To take spots of ink out of silk.—Take strong white wine vinegar and hot ashes, rub them well upon the spots, and afterwards wash with soap and water, and the work will be done.

SILK.

To recover the colour of black silk.—Boil the leaves of a forward summer fig-tree in rain or river water, till a third part of the water is consumed; wash the silk in this water, and then rinse it or brush it over with a little alum water, and it will be restored to a curious fair black.

How to stiffen caffa and the like sorts of silk, and give them a beautiful lustre.—Pound an ounce of gum arabic, and half an ounce of gum tragacanth, very well in a mortar; dissolve them in water; then boil two pounds of linseed in water, so long, till it becomes glutinous; then put in the gum water, make it hot and strain it through a cloth, and, with a sponge, smear it on the wrong side of the silk, taking care that the piece of silk be stretched both in length and breadth, otherwise it will be apt to rumple.

To scent or perfume silks.—After the silk has been dyed, for every pound of silk take an ounce of orris, dry it well. Lay the silks in rose leaves in a thick sieve, and betwixt every row strew powder of orris, and shut it up close in a box or chest, till the next day, and the silk will emit an agreeable odour.

How to keep silk from staining in the washing.—Heat rain water very hot, then put into it Castile soap, dissolve it well; then let it stand till it is almost cold, and then sprinkle in a small quantity of fuller's earth; then scour out the Silks; when you have done, clap them between dry cloths, not suffering them to lie on heaps, and they will look fresh and fair.

To restore silks of any colour that have been soiled or greased.—Take an ounce of unslacked lime, and the like quantity of the ashes of vine-branches, and as much oak-bark; mix them well together in fair water, and make with them a kind of ley, over a gentle fire; let this settle, then take the clear part, and rub over the faded part with a brush or sponge, and it will in a short time restore it.

How to make a soap to take grease, spots, or stains out of silks.—Take roch-alum, burn it well and reduce it to a fine powder, and add to it the powder of the roots of Florentine orris, about half a pound; and to these add a new-laid egg, and two pounds and an half of cake-soap; make them up with fair water into round balls; and, when you would take out any spot or stain, first wash the place well with warm water, and then lay a laying of this soap upon it for three or four hours, and then wash it off with other warm water, and, in often so doing, they will disappear.

To take spots and stains out of very thin silk.—Warm a pint of white-wine vinegar indifferent warm, then dip a black cloth into it, and then rub over the stains; afterwards scrape fuller's earth over them, and clap dry woollen cloths under and over, placing an iron indifferently hot on the upper, and it will draw out the spot etc.

To take spots or stains out of silk.—Bruise an ounce of flax-seeds in two or three spoonfuls of the juice of lemon, and add a quarter of an ounce of white lead, and the same quantity of burnt bone; mix them over a gentle fire to a thickness, and lay them on the strainer.

'A New Universal History of Arts and Sciences.' Vol: II
J. Coote, London, 1759

WEAVING

The English cloth is preferred throughout all Europe, especially the best sorts of all other; though the manufacture of Vanrobes at Abbeville, in Picardy, is arrived to a great degree of perfection; but the French black cloth is preferred to all others for the beauty of the colour.

CAMBLETS: stuff of wool, silk or hair, especially that of goats with wool or wolk; sometimes silk and wool mixed on warp and woof hair. Chiefly made in France, England, Flanders and Holland, Brussels excelling.

Figured Camblets: of one colour, stamped with various figures, flowers, foliages etc. by means of hot irons, which are a kind of moulds, pressed together with the stuff under a press; from Amiens and Flanders, trade in this now less than in the past.

Water Camblets: after weaving, prepared with water and pressed under a hot press, to give them smoothness and lustre.

Waved Camblets: whereon waves are impressed, as on tabbies; by means of a calender, under which they are passed and repassed several times.

The manufacturers of Camblets are to take care they do not acquire any false or needless plaits; it being almost impossible to get them out again.

DRUGGETS: very thin and narrow, usually all wool, sometimes wool and silk. A gold and silver drugget invented by Mr. Savary; the warp partly gold and silver thread, the woof linen.

SERGE: a woollen quilted stuff, woven on four-treddle loom as rateen and other stuffs that have whale. Of several kinds, London Serge is best and most popular abroad. The goodness in Serge is known by the quilting, as that of cloths by the spinning.

RATEEN: thick woollen stuff quilted, woven as serge etc. There are some rateens dressed and prepared like cloth; other left simply in hair, and others where the hair or nap is freezed. Made chiefly in France, Holland and Italy: mostly used in linings.

FRIZE or FREEZE: a woollen cloth for winter wear, being frized or napt on one side. Generally English made frizes are crossed, Irish are not. Freezing cloth is the forming of the nap into a number of little hard burs, almost covering the whole surface. Some cloths, as black, are only freezed on the wrong side; others, coloured and mixed cloths, rateens, bays etc., on the right side.

BAYS: a coarse, open woollen stuff, with a long nap; sometimes frized on one side, according to the use it is intended for; without whale, woven on two-treddle loom like flannel. Made particularly in England, about Colchester, and Flanders, about Lisle and Tourney; now also counterfeited by French at Nimes, Montpelier etc. Exported to Spain, Portugal and Italy. Chiefly used for linings, especially in the army; also behind looking-glasses to preserve the tin or quick-silver, and in lining cases.

FLANEL or FLANNEL: a kind of slight, loose, woollen stuff, not quilted, but very warm. Woven as bays etc.

SAY or SAYE: a kind of serge, or a very light crossed stuff, all wool; much used abroad for linings, and by the Religious for shirts; and in England for Quakers' aprons, for which purpose it is usually green. Made in England near Colchester, exported to Portugal and Leghorn, and also in Flanders.

RIBBAND or RIBBOND: a narrow sort of silk, chiefly used for head-ornaments, badges of chivalry etc. Plain ribbands and figured, all woven in same manner.

TAFFETY or TAFFATY: a fine, smooth silken stuff, with a remarkable lustre or gloss. In all colours, plain, striped with gold, silver, silk etc.; chequered, flowered, in Chinese point, and Hungarian. Chiefly used for summer dresses for women, in linings, scarves, coifs, window curtains etc. Made of specially fine silk, lustre given by water and perfected by passing over fine.

SATTIN or SATIN: a smooth and shining silken stuff, with very fine warp and coarser woof hidden underneath. Both quite plain and wrought, flowered with gold or silk, or striped. Finest are from Genoa and Florence, also Lyons. Bruges satins have silk warp and tread woof. Indian and Chinese satins similar; valued for cleaning and bleaching easily without losing lustre, otherwise inferior to European.

SATTINET or SATTINADE: a slight, thin sort of sattin, chiefly used by ladies for summer night-gowns, and usually striped.

DAMASK: A mixture of mohair and sattin, such that what is not sattin on one side, is on the other. The flowers have a sattin grain, and the ground a grain of taffetas. So named as originating from Damascus.

BROCADE: a cloth of gold, silver or silk, raised and enriched with flowers, foliages etc. Formally name confined to cloth wholly of gold or silver, or both; but came to include silk mixed with this, and at present any stuff of silk, sattin or even simple taffety, when wrought and enriched with flowers, is called brocade.

TABBY: a kind of coarse taffety watered. Made like common taffety, except that it is stronger in both woof and warp. The watering is given by means of a calender, with iron or copper rolls variously engraven; this, bearing unevenly on the stuff, makes the surface unequal to reflect the light differently.

MOHAIR: close-grained stuff, usually all silk; although woof can be of wool, cotton or thread; either smooth and plain, or watered like tabbies.

VELVETS: a rich stuff, all silk, covered on the outside with a close, short fine, solf shag; the other side a very strong close tissue. Made mostly in France and Italy. Many kinds of plain velvets, as well as following:

Figured Velvet: worked with figures, although the ground and figures are both velveted, i.e. the whole surface velvet.

Ramaged or branched Velvet: long stalks, branches etc. on a sattin ground, which is sometimes the same, but more often a different colour with the velvet. Sometimes a gold or silver ground, instead of sattin.

Shorn velvet: when the threads that make the velveting have been ranged in the channelled ruler but not cut there.

Striped Velvet: stripes of various colours, running along the warp; either part sattin, part velvet, or all velveted.

Cut Velvet: has a kind of taffety ground with velvet figures.

HOLLANDS: general name for linnen-cloths, next to Cambrick for fineness; some are even finer than some Cambricks. Made chiefly in Holland.

Guilix Holland: very white and fine; chiefly used for shirts, being the strongest for its fineness of any except true Frieze (made in Frizeland, and is the strongest and best coloured).

Alemaer Holland: very strong and wears exceedingly well. Also linnen made in Brittany, not inferior to Holland and very serviceable. They have brought lately the linnen manufacture to a very great perfection both in Scotland and Ireland.

MUSLIN: a fine sort of cloth, wholly cotton; so called as not being bare, but not having a downy nap on its surface, resembling moss, which the French call Mousse. Various kinds of muslins brought from the East Indies, Chyl, Bengal, Betelles, Tarnatans, Mulmuls, Tangeels, Terrindans, Douas, &c.

Index

replacing hooped, 104; surviving until 1780s, 128; with fringe, cording, etc., ousting laced and galloomed, 27
Quizzing glass, 52, 73

Ramaged velvet, 149
Ramilie-cock hat, x
Rateens, 147
Rayonne, 47
Red coats (m), xii, 52; red heels (m), 25, 51, 52
Reynolds' portraits, 127
Ribbands (fabric), 148
Ribbon coats (slashed), 3
Ribbons, for men, 7, 21, 46 (Pennache); fops', 21; as garters (m), 21; on straw hats (f), 87
Richmond, Duke of, 99
Riding habits, 11; with pinned-back skirts, 73
'Robings' defined, 91
Roll-brim hats, 21
Rolled hair (powdered) of later eighteenth century (f), 112-13
Rolled stockings, 21; outmoded by gartered, 51
'Rollers' (linen stockings with deep lace tops), 1, 6
Rolls in stockings (pads), 25
Rotundity as aim of silhouette, in 1710s, 70
Roundabout aprons, 62
Round gowns, introduction of, 136; in the 1790s, 136, 140
Rowlandson, T., 134
Royal occasion described (1792), 136-8
Ruching introduced, 106
Ruffles (m), xi, 3, 14, 94, 95; persistence of, on shirts, 123; on women's outdoor coats after 1750, 109; see also p. 45, 'Engageants'
Rump jewels, 36, 62, 63

Sac (Sack), i.e. 'contouche', gown with full-gathered back, 10, 70; French-style, 83; in 1730s, 86, 87, 88; in 1748, 78, 92; in late eighteenth century, 101; short form of, 88;

with matching petticoat as enduring fashion, 104; mainly designed for hoops, 101
Sailor's dress, 97
St. James Coffee House, 64
St. Jean, J. O. de, 21
Sandby, Paul, 101
Sashes (m), 21, 23; (f) 134, 140
Sat(t)in, 148; for embroidered waistcoats (m), 93
Sattinade (Sattinet), 148
Savary's gold-and-silver drugget (fabric), 147
Say (saye) (fabric), 148
Say and Seale (i.e. Saye and Sele), Lady, 99
Scarborough, Lady, 80, 91
Scarlet: coats, xii, 52; stockings, 18, 51
School for Husbands (Molière), 5
Scotch caps, Glengarry type (f), 87
Scouring of clothes, 99, 132
Selwyn, George, 107
Sequins, as embroidery embellishment (m), 93, 117, 119, 135
Serge, 147
Shape as period dress criterion, x, 70
Shifts (garment under stays), 11, 12; frilled, with wadded waistcoat, 70; frill of disappears, 64; see Kerchiefs, Tuckers, as replacing shift frill; shift frill, 11, 64, 70
Shirts: laced, ruffled (Charles II), 3; early eighteenth-century frilled-front, 51; for Religious, 148; sleeve shapes of, 3, 6; elaborate, of 1660-80, 3-6; see Waistcoats, as sleeved waistcoats early assume some functions of shirts.
Shirtwaisted: cutaway coats (m), 122; waistcoats (m), 122
Shoes: buckled (m), 25; square-toed (m), with high heels, 14, 25; buckled high-heeled (m), 21; embroidered laced over-shoes (f), 62; laced, i.e. covered with lace, 60, 62, 63; long, narrow, high-red-heeled (m), 25; with pointed, turned-up toe (f), 62; superseded by boots for most occasions, 119
Shorn velvet, 149